The First Year

of Mukdar

Lloyd Harradan and Ramdath Jagessar

Excerpts from Mukdar, the pioneering Indian
resistance and revival magazine in Trinidad,
in its first year of operation 1974.

Toronto, Canada 2009

Contents

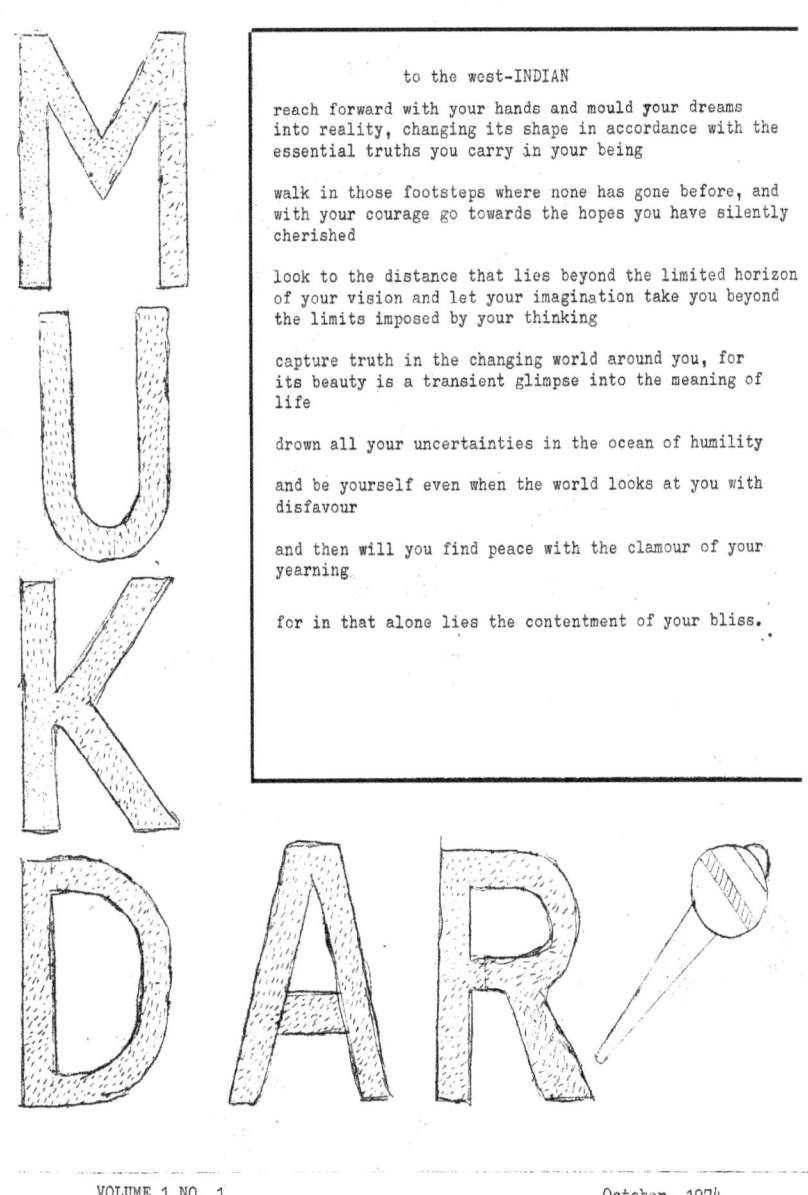

to the west-INDIAN

reach forward with your hands and mould your dreams
into reality, changing its shape in accordance with the
essential truths you carry in your being

walk in those footsteps where none has gone before, and
with your courage go towards the hopes you have silently
cherished

look to the distance that lies beyond the limited horizon
of your vision and let your imagination take you beyond
the limits imposed by your thinking

capture truth in the changing world around you, for
its beauty is a transient glimpse into the meaning of
life

drown all your uncertainties in the ocean of humility

and be yourself even when the world looks at you with
disfavour

and then will you find peace with the clamour of your
yearning

for in that alone lies the contentment of your bliss.

VOLUME 1 NO. 1   October, 1974

The cover of the first issue of MUKDAR, October 1974

3

Introduction

We chose the magazine's name Mukdar from the saying "pull the mukdar" that was common in Indian settlements in Trinidad during the 1970's. The mukdar is the mace or war club usually seen with the Hindu deity Lord Hanuman, the great defender of Lord Rama and Mother Sita.

When important matters came to a breaking point without a solution in sight, someone would say "time to pull the mukdar!". It meant time for action, time to fight for your rights and your survival. "Pull the mukdar" was the message we wanted to bring to the half million strong Indian community in Trinidad and the extended Indian community of over a million in the Caribbean.

When Mukdar appeared in October 1974 it had been another bad year for the Indian community, the 18th bad year in a row. In 1956 the Indians had lost the contest for political power to the black (called negro at the time) political party the People's National Movement. From that time the PNM had identified Indians as the political enemy and launched a campaign to keep themselves in power permanently by destroying the Indians as a group. They started rigging the elections and flooding the country with illegal blacks from other Caribbean islands, all to keep Indians out of power.

The PNM ravaged the economic base of the Indians by just abandoning the country areas where most Indians lived. They allowed agriculture, the mainstay of Indians, to slowly wither away. The government took control of most of the economy, and spent most of the budget on urban areas where the blacks lived. Most state jobs, state built housing, utilities like water, electricity, telephones, sewerage facilities, went to blacks. Massive discrimination in hiring kept Indians out of employment in many areas of government work.

Indians in the rural areas generally lived without without proper electricity, water, roads, access roads for agriculture, telephones, recreation facilities, and libraries. There were few secondary schools, primitive health facilities, no cottage industries, and very little in the way of agricultural development. Unemployment among rural Indians was enormous. The Indian heartland was a huge wasteland in a country floating on oil wealth, much of it taken from those same rural areas that saw little of the wealth coming back to them. Growing numbers of Indians were quietly abandoning the richest country in the Caribbean to seek their fortunes and their survival elsewhere

Added to the political and economic battering of the Indians was a concerted assault on Indian culture and identity. Socially, the Indians became the whipping boy in Trinidad. The blacks told us we were clannish, not modern, unpatriotic, greedy for money and racist for refusing to intermarry with them to to form a new race,

Indian culture was considered an inferior foreign culture that should be eliminated. The PNM government described the country as a land of calypso, steelband and Carnival which was essentially the culture of the blacks. Indian food, Indian music, Indian films, Indian names, Indian religions like Hinduism and Islam were scorned and marked out for elimination.

Indian males were pictured as weak and unmanly, lacking confidence and social graces, and sexually laughable with our little, soft penises. We Indians didn't know how to dress, how to dance, how to eat good strong food, how to talk to people. They told us we were a bunch of drunkards and wife beaters, quick to commit suicide when the going got tough. We were not modern, not bold, not sexy, not in tune with the new music.

In the schools and work places we were mocked for having comical old fashioned Indian names like Beharrylal and Chandradaye, for putting coconut oil in our hair and bringing roti and pumpkin for lunch instead of bread and ham. The blacks pitied us for not knowing the latest calypsoes, the latest dance steps, and what was happening in the Carnival camps. To be Indian in Trinidad in that time was to know that you were despised by the rest of the society.

Black Trinidad found there was little that was good or admirable about the Indians in Trinidad, nothing for the country to learn from. It was better that most things Indian were swept away and replaced with something that was created by the negro rulers of Trinidad. We Indians had become throw away people placed in the dumpster ready for disposal.

The other ethnic groups such as the white Europeans, the Chinese, the Syrian-Lebanese, the mixed-race group, all said nothing about the Indian genocide proceeding in front of their eyes. Nearly all of them joined the PNM.

The PNM had succeeded in breaking off some elements from the Indian community. The leadership of the Muslims and most of the membership joined the PNM, and much the same happened with the Presbyterian Indians. Some of the Hindu groups like the Arya Pratinidhi Sabha, even some leaders of the main Hindu body the Sanatan Dharma Maha Sabha, were clearly joining an anti Indian, anti

Hindu political party. They were all silent on the party's political, economic and cultural genocide policies towards Indians.

The bulk of the Indian middle class and professional group of business people, lawyers, doctors, academics and the like, just abandoned the mass of grass roots Indians to their fate. Many joined the PNM party that was openly targeting their own people, and tried to distance themselves from their country cousins, the humble and oppressed Indians.

In the open the ordinary Indian stood alone, taking blows from all sides, abandoned even by his own natural leaders. He had no political party, no human rights group, no religious group, no racial group, no intellectual boldly taking up his cause. Nobody spoke up for him, so it was no surprise that he was deep in despair and self hatred. Some Indians were starting to deny their very identity, claiming that they were "not Indian but Trinidadian". It became trendy to put down behaviour that was "too Indian". There seemed no reason to be proud to be an Indian or a Hindu in Trinidad.

Trinidad Indians in 1974 were for all purposes a beaten race. Politically, socially, economically, culturally, psychologically, we were lost. The ordinary Indian had been told he was nothing and could feel he was nothing. He didn't understand what was happening to him or what were the intentions of those delivering his punishment.

We had no plans for resistance, nor any ideas on how to resist. Relentless enemies from the outside and selfish traitors from the inside had weakened the Indians to the point of surrender. We had no idea of the existence of thousands of Indians in over ten Caribbean countries, most of whom were in a worse condition than the Trinidadian Indians.

We had little solidarity with our Guyanese cousins being crushed by the black racist dictator Forbes Burnham with massive support from Guyanese blacks.

Facing us was the mass of blacks giving overwhelming support to the PNM, the other groups also supporting the blacks, and an international world that had no interest in our plight. Even the ambassadors from India wanted to have nothing to do with our troubles.

Truly, this was the time to "pull the mukdar". It was time to raise up the will to resist the black onslaught, to begin an Indian revival.

Lloyd Harradan and Krishna Gannesingh, two young graduates of the University of the West Indies, hatched the idea for Mukdar, and Ramdath Jagessar joined up soon after. The plan was simple- start doing something, anything, to head off the agenda of Indian destruction. We would use our own resources, and seek no approval or financial backers to publish an Indian resistance and cultural revival magazine.

We became the editors and main writers of Mukdar, which was launched very quietly in October 1974. It was launched quietly and distributed only to Indians because that was a time when any statement of Indian identity was seen as racism, viewed by non-Indians as a kind of treason. From the first Mukdar was an underground paper that was shown only to sympathetic Indians, and never to blacks.

Our plan was very simple. Say what was the situation facing Indians and what was causing it. Identify the enemies of Indians, their motives and their methods, and expose them. Identify the enemies of Indians within the Indian community. and target them. Find out what was happening to the other Indians in the Caribbean and build up

8

Caribbean contacts and solidarity. Develop the arguments for Indians to use against our enemies. Show that positive value of Indian culture and the Indian heritage. Work to help the ordinary Indian feel pride in himself and our people. Reject any plans for Indian people that did not have majority Indian support. Stay far away from the politicians and the established Indian leaders in Trinidad.

Mukdar had no funders, financiers, or wealthy backers. Copies were sold in the beginning, and occasionally there would be small donations, but generally the editors funded Mukdar out of their own pockets. They wrote it, typed out the stencils, ran off the copies on Gestetner copiers, assembled and stapled by hand, and distributed it with the help of volunteers. After some attempts, the Mukdar editors gave up on trying to get financial help from the many wealthy Indians around. Business and professional Indians were usually terrified of being associated with something like Mukdar. Most of the time they refused to help and some would strenuously discourage the printing of Mukdar because they thought it would cause trouble.

But the reception to Mukdar from the ordinary grass roots Indians was tremendous. They had long wanted something speaking from the heart, speaking for Indians without apologies and cringing, identifying the enemies and friends of Indians, laying out the issues without fear. This was something the Indian politicians, middle class and professionals had never done and could not do. Mukdar was the seed of Indian revolution, Indian revival, Indian resistance.

But Mukdar was not without risk for the editors and supporters. Occasionally the blacks would hear of the existence of a "racist Indian newspaper" that was attacking them and their government, but so few ever saw a Mukdar that it never went anywhere. Indians who got their hands on one would never share it with black colleagues at work or black friends if they had any.

On one occasion we heard that the Attorney General Karl Hudson Phillips was informed of the racist Indian newspaper Mukdar. He asked Indian lawyers in his office if Mukdar should be investigated and prosecuted. Thankfully, the Indian lawyers told him that Mukdar was insignificant and had no support, so it wasn't worth the attention. For that we thank them.

This is just the first volume of excerpts from Mukdar. The magazine ran for five years, and there is more to come. What was the significance of Mukdar we will never know. What we do know is that some of the ideas and perceptions put out in Mukdar struck a deep chord in the Indian community in Trinidad. Other magazines and groups formed in the Indian community soon after, political figures rose up in the community, cultural activists, religious movements in the Hindu community, and an Indian revival coincided with the years of Mukdar.

That was more than 30 years ago. We were young men and women then, angry young men and women not willing to stay silent while our people were destroyed. We did what we could to save a desperate situation, and can only hope we helped our Indian community to a better place than it was in 1974. If there's still a need to pull the Mukdar in Trinidad today, another generation will have to do it.

Lloyd Harradan & Ramdath Jagessar
(Krishna Ganeesingh is deceased)

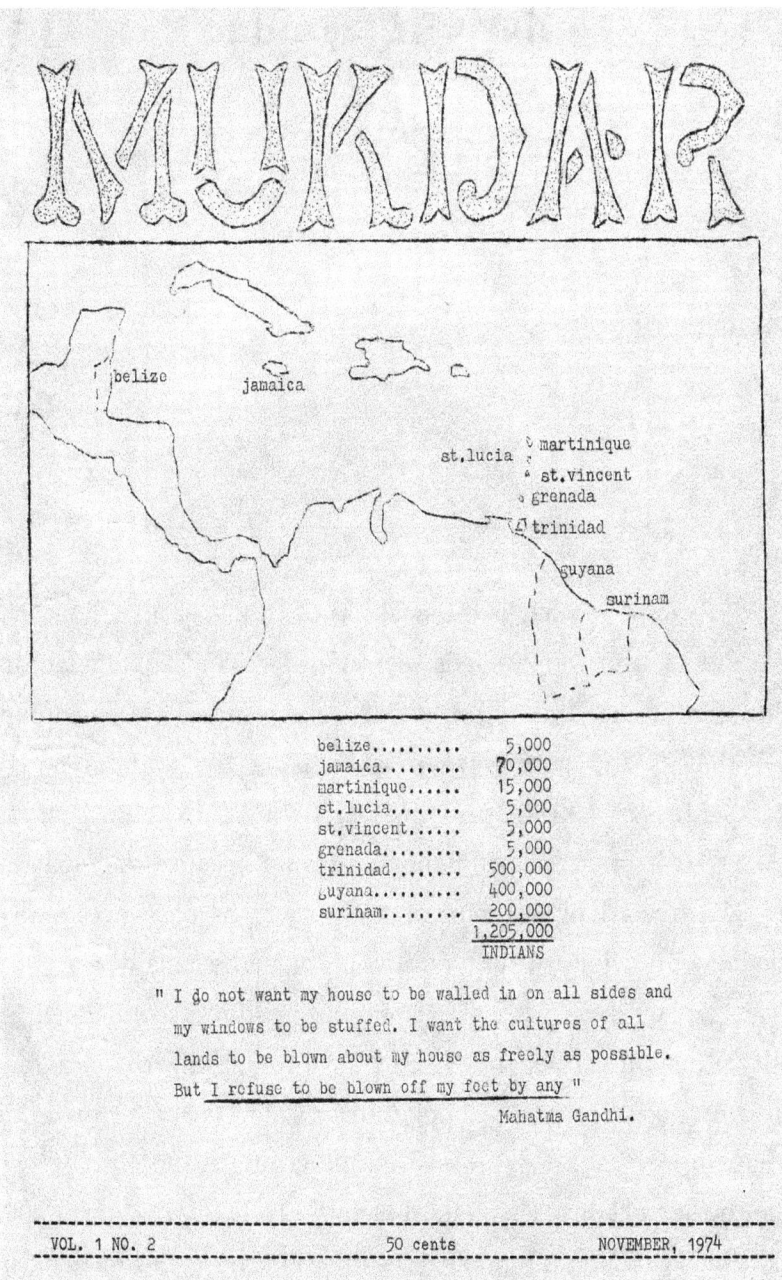

belize......... 5,000
jamaica......... 70,000
martinique...... 15,000
st.lucia........ 5,000
st.vincent...... 5,000
grenada......... 5,000
trinidad........ 500,000
guyana.......... 400,000
surinam......... 200,000
1,205,000
INDIANS

" I do not want my house to be walled in on all sides and
my windows to be stuffed. I want the cultures of all
lands to be blown about my house as freely as possible.
But I refuse to be blown off my feet by any "

Mahatma Gandhi.

VOL. 1 NO. 2   50 cents   NOVEMBER, 1974

The cover of the November 1974 Mukdar

Indians in Trinidad

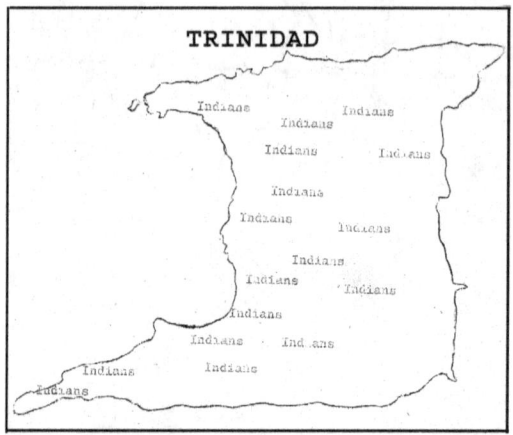

Exactly in what is the position of Indians in Trinidad is a question we must try to answer before making conclusions or solutions for the "Indian problem." As a group, how do Indians fare, that is the entire group comprising town and country, Hindu, Muslim, Christian, non-religious, businessmen, farmers, workers? We must take Indians as a group because they exist as one, are treated by the rest of the society as one. Economics, housing, education, culture, politics, all must be considered.

Let us start with the economic position, from which so many other things depend. Here I have to agree with economist Winston Dookeran in the book "From Calcutta to Caroni", that Indians are the most depressed ethnic group in the society. For, despite the very few visible and wealthy Indians, the group as a whole lags well behind the negroes in economic well-being.

In general, they get less jobs in proportion to their share

of the population, their jobs are worse paid, they have to spend more on travel, have bigger families and less food to feed them with. Their education levels are lower, they have inferior water, lights, roads, sewerage, health facilities, have less amenities for sport, recreation, less libraries.

They get less of the government houses, government jobs, scholarships, jobs as a whole. They're sicker, commit more suicide, see more of their children becoming prostitutes and have much less influence in making economic decisions, whether private or government, that other ethnic groups.

In case this sound strange to ears accustomed to talk of Indian prosperity let us look at some of the facts.

Indians, who were 36.5% of the population in 1960, live mainly in the country, 70 percent of them being country dwellers as compared to 44 percent of the negroes. As a whole Indians are over 50 percent of the country population and over 21 percent of the town population (where negroes are over 50 percent). So it would be safe to say the position of the country (areas) gives an idea of the position of the Indians in general.

Only 36 percent of country homes have pipe borne water to 80% in the town, and in 0.3% have sewerage facilities, to 50% in the towns. Leo Pujadas of the Central statistical Office has pointed out that town people have more money as well. 1974 figures show that 60 percent of town households have an average income of over $200 a month, compared to to 87% for country households, which also have one more persons per family on the average. Average spending per month for town homes is $370 but only $278 for the country, which in addition spends more of its money on transport and fuel. Those from the country who have jobs often have to travel long distances, eating away their take-home pay.

The food of the rural people is poorer, more deficient in protein, one major reason for the greater extent of illness. They spend 42.8% of their food money on basic foods like rice and flour and only 17 percent on meat compared to to 33% and 23.7% respectively for the towns. They have to spend their money on bulk food that fills them up but are not rich in protein. It is therefore no surprise that so many chronic cases of sickness in our hospitals, particularly tuberculosis, are Indians from the country. The country also has the worst of the normal facilities like water, sewage etc.

Over 80 percent of secondary schools are located in town, meaning the meaning expensive travel for country children who also have to do things like cut grass, graze animals, plant crops and fill water. Country children are the ones you see standing up long hours in the taxi and bus stands waiting to get home, the ones who don't do so well in sports because there are no facilities where they live. Most of the National Housing Authority schemes are placed in town, and as we all know, the houses are given mainly to negroes. Special works projects seem to cling to the town areas, and even visual checks will show the vast majority of negroes getting the jobs.

Since the negroes are 38 percent of the rural population they tend to suffer some of the fate reserve for Indians. But observers have noticed that lights, water, better roads that Indian dominated areas (are) very near to them. When we look at the overall situation, Indians to negroes, we see that again our people are way behind as far as the economy is concerned.

In 1968 Indians were 36.5% of the population but only 31% while the negroes were 43.3% of the population and 49 percent of the labour force. That is equality for you. Indian workers were 25 percent of the Indian population and negro workers were 36% of the negro population. When you took out the unpaid workers Indian paid workers became 25% of the Indian population and negroes 35% of their population. Quite simply the negroes got more than their share of the job according to their share of the population. Up to the present time the negroes are screaming how unequaled they are in comparison to the whites, but they don't care how unequal compared to them.

In 1970 the average monthly income of Indians was $156, the negroes $194 and the average $190. If we assume the majority of agricultural workers are Indian then it is no surprise that the 1971 median income of agriculture was $142 for government and $84 for the private sector. The median income is what most of the people get in reality, in comparison to the , which can be very misleading. For example if 30 people get $1 a day and five get $8 a day average for the 35 would be $2 a day, while the media would be $1, since that is what most people get.

Still, the average can be useful, as when we see Caroni saying that male sugar workers (Indian naturally) get an average of $117 a month and women $56.80 a month. The average for the civil service or teaching will of course be something different, but then so many negroes are in those professions. These same urban negroes were so indifferent or unsympathetic when sugar workers were fighting for guaranteed work so they wouldn't starve six months of the year.

Indians who were 36.5% of the people were only 31 percent of the labour force and got only 25 percent of the wage bill. The negroes got 50 percent (of the wage bill) and the "other connection, the non Indian/non negro sector, who were only 20 percent of the labour force got 25 percent of the wage bill in 1960. As Choko would say, would you believe this has changed? Not likely.

26.1 percent of Indians have no education, to 2.5% of negroes, 66.4% have primary education only to 87.2% for negroes, and 7.5 percent have post primary education, to 10.35% for negroes. 7% of the business elite are Indians, according to Acton Camejo's report, better than the 4% of negroes. However, 78% of the negro group were promoted into the elite class, to 63 percent of the white/off- white group -and a mere 15 percent of Indians.. That is as clear sign of the future as one can want.

The government, the biggest employer and spender of our billion dollar budgets and oil revenue, sees fit not to spend it equally on Indians and negroes. There is only one word for it, racial discrimination no matter how we try to cover it up as industrial development. We can also note that despite a world food crisis, spiralling food prices in Trinidad and the decline of agriculture, government has refused to develop a real agricultural policy or give a serious boost to agriculture.

Sure Indians will benefit but so will the whole country be getting cheaper local food. But there is simply no logical reason for the neglect of agriculture, especially now, but we are sure this neglect will continue even if bodi goes up to $1 a bundle.

But anyone can notice how many Indians are in the police, army, higher ranks of the civil service, how many get scholarships. There are other aspects of life than the economic- such as of our culture, our placed in politics, the respect given to our people.

Culturally the Indian is under intense attack, aimed at destroying him as a cultural entity, at removing his Indianness. Leading the onslaught is the PNM itself with the tacit or open support of the majority of negroes, no matter what the political views of those negroes are. The PNM's motives are the same as those of the masters who deculturised the negro slaves. Indians have always been the base of opposition to the PNM, which seeks to destroy all opposition as we we all know. Therefore it plans to destroy the Indian as a group, and what unites them as a group, their culture and racial togetherness.

Integration is the weapon to achieve this; cultural integration which should force us to give up our culture and become creole, so we look up to our cultural creole "masters" instead of opposing them. Racial integration, the so-called merging of Indians and negroes to form a third race, is supposed to douglarise the Indian and ensure that there is no person who can claim to be a "pure" Indian or negro. If there is no Indian community they will be no Indian problem, reason these idiots, and PNM will rule forever. They don't care that they will be no negro community either - in fact they welcome that, so ashamed they of their negroness and so anxious to get away from their blackness.

The PNM feels that if there is no Indian culture to unite the Indians then Indians as a body will not oppose the PNM. After all you do not fight the people you are trying to imitate, the exponents of the "national religion" of calypso, Carnival and steelband. Racially there will be no one who is clearly Indian, so Indian consciousness of the kind I'm expressing here will not be a problem. In other words we will lose our pedigree and become a race of mongrels - a race of douglas, if we can grace douglas with the world race. This absurd policy suits the negroes quite well, as they're generally ashamed of their race and will do anything to merge with any other race, even with the Indians whom they profess to despise.

This policy of theirs is dangerous because it does get them some results. Indians who are culturally creole often prefer negroes to their own people, are heard to attack Indian culture regularly, and are not very hostile to the racist PNM. They don't give a damn for Indians as a group and ignore racial attacks on the part of negroes as if they were pranks of spoiled children. Douglas usually identify with negroes rather than Indians, as is well known.

However this situation has not advanced very far yet, and we are glad to see that integration is one of the main targets of the militant Indian groups that the beginning to spring up. According to our reports they have found a good response, in spite of the many years of propaganda about merging of cultures and racial harmony put out by the negroes.

Groups have started commenting that only steelband is being pushed as Trinidad culture, that the Tourist Board shows Trinidad to be a land of negroes, that 'Ambakaila' is being touted as representative of our culture though it has little or nothing Indian about it. We know that government has been pressuring firms to sponsor steel bands and completely ignoring the Indian orchestras who flourish better than negro (orchestras) in spite of repression. But while it is obvious that resistance to the creole trend is growing a number of Indians are still caught in the trap of giving up their culture.

They don't see that for the negroes, creole culture is Trinidad culture and what the vast Indian section feels doesn't count. They coolly ignore the way of life of over 40 percent of the population, and still feel they are not discriminating against us, or worse than that, that we are discriminating against them.

This may be the reason why Indians do not feel Trinidadian except in the geographical sense. We were born here but apart from that-nothing, for when we see a Trinidadian defined we cannot recognize ourselves in that hip shaking, bacchanal loving, live for today person. We note moves being made to teach steelband and calypso in schools, why our thing is left out and Hindi, a living language of thousands, is bypassed for Spanish, French and even dead Latin.

The press, radio, TV advertisers, all push creole culture or American culture, and care nothing for our culture.

Racial integration is accepted by almost all the blacks, who are firm in their desire for a third "race" of douglas, who are really no racer at all. Despite the negro contempt for Indians the blacks are insisting and demanding that we intermarry with them. Why does a group of people who like to boast of being black and proud want to mix with a group of people they do not respect?

The truth is that they feel their race is inferior, the worst of all the races and want to get away from it. This is why the negro men are rushing at our women, doing anything to get an Indian girl so that their children will only be half negro, their grandchildren less and maybe future descendants not negro at all.

Their women want the same thing but are frustrated because Indian men do not want them, and they're ashamed to go chasing after them, so they act as sour grapes and say they don't like Indian men anyway. Indian men prefer their own people-a lesson the negroes have yet to learn. No other racial or ethnic group in the word is anxious to lose their identity except the Caribbean and American negroes. Apart from the political reason this is the cause why negroes are practically demanding that we give them our women and accusing us of being racial if we refuse.

We have had political and economic discrimination for years now and cultural integration for some time too, but the recent upsurge in racial integration poses the greatest danger, if only because it is visible. We can see it, and every new mixed couple is interpreted by the negroes as a victory for them and a defeat for us. It is a good thing that at last some of our young people a beginning to openly reject this integration policy, for it is time this trend is severely questioned. Racial mixing has not been shown to provide any advantages and this will not solve when it goes together with racism against the non integrating Indians.

We are also hearing about the problems faced by Indian girls who marry negro men, noted for their irresponsibility and poor qualities as fathers, to find themselves deserted, with children they cannot support and unable to go back to their parents. It is not too late to examine integration carefully, and if necessary reject it totally as it is being pushed.

Overall we see two trends: One one is the trend we know so well, the creolizing, integrating, giving up culture trend that is particularly favored by the urban Indians, Christian Indians and professionals who want to go up in the social ladder.

The next is a more heartening trend, of Indians becoming militant, going back to our culture and fighting for its preservation and modernization of our ancient heritage. Some who were already halfway gone are coming back when they see that creolizing doesn't help them or their people very much. They see that in the eyes of negroes they gain little, as the blacks remain as biased and anti-Indian as ever. More important, they are starting to talk, write, form groups and spread the word. And since many of them are quite intelligent and aggressive they are adding a new tone to a situation. Something very different to be cringing defense of the older generation.

They are not only defending us, but are attacking the flimsy arguments put up by the negroes for their racial policies. And make no mistake, the negroes will see what is happening are scared of these young bold young Indians who are not afraid to accuse the PNM and so many negroes of racism instead of quietly suffering the same charges themselves.

At the same time the pro-negro trend is stronger, as they have years of experience and all the money to spend on it, but no matter how hard you push it a wrong policy is a wrong policy and will collapse when put to the test of fire. The pro-Indian trend, while small and just developing, will surely grow much more powerful in the near. It certainly does not lack support from the Indians who have felt discrimination for so long.

The victory of Basdeo Panday's sugar workers has shown Indians can fight and win, and the message is gaining strength. Krishna Gowandan has accused the TIWU (Transport and Industrial Workers Union) of racism, Jack Kelshall has hit the PNM and OWTU (Oilfield Workers Trade Union) for racial discrimination against Indians, while Indian intellectuals are saying the same thing in many quarters, like MUKDAR for example. We are coming to the end of the rope.

The pro- Indians will inevitably become stronger, as more Indians see that playing the negro game doesn't help them. As one friend pout it, "We stay quiet and we still get kicked, so staying quiet is not the answer." Superficially this situation seems the same but below change is already visible for those who can see-and soon will become painfully obvious even for those who do not want to see.

....

HERE AND THERE:

BLACK BOARD FOR BLACK GOLD

The Right Honorable Eric surely has a sense of propriety. What could be more appropriate than a black board for the black gold company? Eric has been out of school so long, perhaps he does not know they painting blackboards green now. The whole thing stinks Eric. Even more than the National Awards.

(Prime Minister Dr Eric Williams had just appointed a new board for the national oil company composed of 100% black directors and no Indians.)

POETRY

My soul has no voice

Miss Narindei Naraysingh from Jamaica

Let me tell you a tale
But listen with your heart
For my soul has no voice.

Can you hear
Anguish
In a lonely tear
As it trickles sadly
Down
Cheeks of despair?

Listen to my laughter
Of mimicked happiness
The sorrow-tinted tones
In its ringing mirth

Listen to the pulsating rhythm
Of the swan-song's melody
In my heart

Listen to my silent screams
Of futile rebellion

The voices of fears, frustration
And hear my secret dreams
Strangled
Before their journey's end

Listen
Listen well
For my soul
Has no voice

-   2   -

How can I
Write my soul
On a bit of paper?

How can I record
A dream?

Dreams are elusive
they have wings
they fly away
But they return
To fly away...again

And how can I
Tell of wounds

That never bled
But left scars?

Scars have a numbing effect
They numb your mind
They wither your soul

What empty bliss
Not to feel
Not to care
Not to yearn

What horror
To be dead...
While alive

(Editor's Comments:
In these two poems, Miss Naraysingh, who no longer resides in
Jamaica, has captured the despair and tragedy of the Indian in
Jamaica...the laughter that is a mimicry of happiness, secret
dreams that are strangled, dreams that fly away, wounds on the
psychological make-up of the Indian that left scars on their
personalities.)

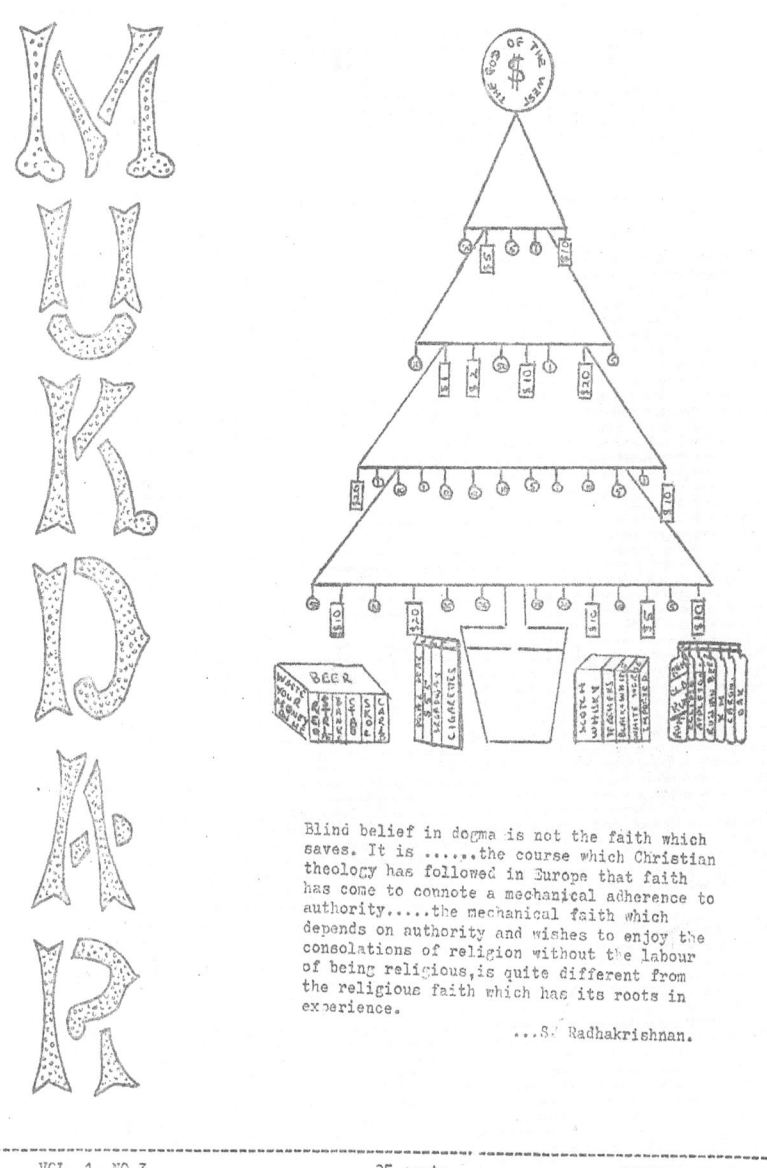

Blind belief in dogma is not the faith which saves. It is ......the course which Christian theology has followed in Europe that faith has come to connote a mechanical adherence to authority.....the mechanical faith which depends on authority and wishes to enjoy the consolations of religion without the labour of being religious,is quite different from the religious faith which has its roots in experience.

...S. Radhakrishnan.

VOL. 1. NO.3   25 cents   DECEMBER,1974

The cover of the December 1974 MUKDAR

Indians in Guyana

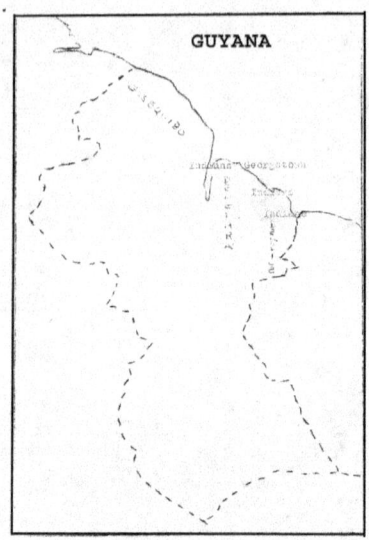

Guyana Council of Indian Organizations

September 3, 1974

At this moment of great distress for Guyana, your assistance is sought in order that a tragedy of unimaginable proportions may be averted in this dear land of ours.

A world economic crisis has descended upon Guyana already weakened by racism and corruption. A select elite has imposed itself upon an unwilling and unhappy people by the force of arms and under the protection of these, is engaged in extensive looting and pillaging of the nation's resources.

This elite, represented in a political party called People's

National Congress installed itself at a fraudulent elections on July 16th, 1973 and as it did prior to the so called elections, is using racial propaganda combined with a subtle blend of ethnic discrimination and favoritism to perpetuate its imposition upon the people.

Corruption is another cancer to which the nation is subject. This is now institutionalized and has become part of the way of life of the Guyanese people. Honesty is now a distinct liability and public morality at all levels has hit the bottom of the country. The attendant vices of fraud and prostitution are widespread.

Freedom to speak, to think, to listen and read have disappeared. The press and radio are totally subservient to the regime and now serve up news which is doctored, tailored, slanted and fabricated to satisfy its needs.

The new elite is living in great luxury and affluence and each member is striving to become an overnight millionaire while the masses are called upon to make all the sacrifices.

We attach a memorandum which we hope you shall find useful in understanding the problem.

We would welcome your support in resisting the injustice which prevails in Guyana and would also welcome a visit by your representative to examine conditions at first hand.

Yours sincerely,

M Azad Khan (P.R.O. of the Guyana Council of Indian Organizations

Memorandum
Guyana-a victim of racism.

We have tried to submit from below some facts and figures to indicate the extent of racial discrimination which is being practiced by a minority clique against the Guyanese of Indian descent who form the majority of the population. In fact the picture is not dissimilar to that of Rhodesia and other parts of Southern Africa. There is merely a reversal of roles.

It does appear that the South African regimes are attacked by Guyana's hierarchy in order to provide a smokescreen for the introduction of the very racist techniques into this country.

Population:

The Guyana population of 750,000 is made up as follows

Indians	-55%
Africans	-33%
Amerindians	-8%
Europeans	-1%
Chinese	-1%
Mixed	-4%

Elections:

The ballot box is no longer allowed to express the free will of the people. General elections held in Guyana on the 16th day of

July, 1973, were easily the most fraudulent in the history of the Eastern Caribbean. Indeed the Catholic Standard, the official organ of the powerful Catholic Church in Guyana describe them as "Fairy Tale" Elections. There was the clearest evidence of massive irregularities including the seizure, impounding and tampering with the ballot boxes by the military who in effect staged a coup d'etat to maintain their the ruling People's National Congress government in office. Some of the techniques used by the People's National Congress to rig itself into office are set out hereunder:-

(a) Padding of the voters list which was increased in 1973 by 24.5% over the last list in 1968. Yet official government statistics showed an average population increase of only 2.5 percent per year.

(b) The entire voter registration and electoral machinery was manned by an almost 100% People's National Congress personnel-500 specially selected Africans.

(c) The innovation of the postal vote which was used to enable fictitious names appearing on the voters list, to vote.

(d) The scandalous abuse of proxy voting e.g. even though the last day for the making of applications to vote by proxy was 10 days before voting day, successful applications were being made made even on Polling Day. There were numerous instances of forged applications.

(e) The refusal of the Election Commission to discharge its constitutional obligation of ensuring the fairness and impartiality of the elections .

(f) The unwarranted armed intervention of the Guyana Defense Force in the conduct of the elections. The army commandeered the ballot boxes in relation to all opposition strongholds, took them to army headquarters where they were broken into, and ballots removed and replaced by suitably pre-marked ballots.

(g) Contrary to an agreement reached with the Chief Elections Officer, permissions were refused for one representative of the opposition parties to accompany the ballot boxes to their places of destination.

Corruption:

The Director of Audit reported in 1969 that a total of $20 million of the nation's funds were not accounted for during 1967 and he was promptly relieved of his responsibilities. It is obvious that there was fraud at all levels .

His successor has been unable until very recently to submit reports on the state of public funds for 1968. The picture is not at all dissimilar.

Press and radio:

The press and radio are for the most part completely subservient to the regime, and the solitary newspaper which dares to criticize it faces the possibility that newsprint supplies (which have to be imported under license) will be cut off. This paper has had to interrupt its publication on three occasions during the last two years for varying periods because of failure to obtain licenses for newsprint. One Government minister said recently there must be constant scrutiny of the press and radio.

Public Service:

The highest career public servants are the permanent secretaries of whom there are 18 as heads of the various government ministries and they are responsible to the politically appointed minister. There is only one Indian among the 18.

The merit principle has had to give way to racial considerations and senior Indian public servants are being superseded or hounded out of the government service. In addition to the permanent secretaries each government department has a technical head. There are 28 such heads of whom only two are Indian.

Military and Police Force:

Africans form 95% of the armed forces and police in the

country and East Indians have been deliberately excluded in order that "Racial muscle" could be made available to the government to terrorize the population. Because these disciplined services do not reflect the ethnic composition of the population, they do not enjoy their confidence. The International Commission of Jurists which visited Guyana in 1965 recommended that more Indians should be introduced into these services but instead the government sought to reduce the number. On one occasion not long ago when 300 persons were taken into the police force one turned out to be an Indian.

Government Corporations:

Besides government departments proper, there are 22 statutory government corporations, each being responsible for a field of activity e.g. Airways, Marketing, Printing, Electricity, Broadcasting, etc. Not a single one of the 22 heads of the corporations is an Indian, and only 5% of the work force is Indian.

Economic:

The rice, copra and milk industries which have been developed by the Indians and are mostly run by them are in a state of depression because the government thinks that this is a useful way to keep the Indians at starvation level, and "break" them economically.

The government as part of its policy has nationalized

several operations since it came to office in 1964, e.g. Broadcasting, Printing, Bauxite, etc. But the motivation is not really socialism but rather as a means to displace the Indians and to find work for its own supporters. That explains why all these enterprises have only a 5% Indian content at the present time.

As another example of the cruel injustice meted out to Indians, we may state that when the government decided to organize public transportation, it bought new buses and gave jobs to its own party members.

Those Indians who owned the buses which operated routes previously were merely given short notices to quit the road. No compensation was offered and their buses were left to rot. Both the owners and their creditors lost large sums of money as a result.

Because unemployment affects the Indians more than other communities the young Indian boys are resorting to crime and the girls to prostitution.

Land distribution:

The Indians are largely a farming community but in keeping with Government's policy, they are denied land to farm. These lands are distributed mostly to the Africans even though this community has shown little interest in agricultural enterprises.

Social Security:

The entire Social Security apparatus both at the central and local levels are in the hands of the PNC and it is noted that even the aged Indian has a hard time receiving old age benefits. The African has no such difficulty.

Religious:

The government has been interfering with religious organizations and has been sparing no pains to bring them under its control. This attitude results in a denial of religious freedom with the banning of popular Hindu and Muslim organizations from conducting religious broadcasts and the prevention of missionaries from entering the country. A Trinidad Hindu choir of 30 was refused entry last year to Guyana.

Cultural:

The government's cultural agency, the History and Arts Council which is under the control of the Minister of Information and Culture has a membership of 29 of whom six are East Indians, the result being that the Indian aspects of Guyanese culture received no government support or encouragement.

There a re two broadcasting stations, one being state owned, and yet they are allowed to offer only one hour of Indian music each, during the course of an 18 hour broadcast day. Indians have to listen to neighboring Surinam for Indian cultural programs.

Government facilities are not made available for Indian cultural functions, as part of the government's campaign to discourage this type of cultural activity.

Judiciary:

There have been instances recently of racial manipulation of the jury system resulting in a denial of justice.

Ombudsman:

This office was created with much pomp and it was felt that it would ensure racial justice and clean government. But even this office has now become non-functional. There has been no report of its activities since 1969.

In 1971 the ombudsmen investigated two complaints from members of the public about alleged acts of corruption committed by two Ministers of the Government. No report on the investigation, which came to an end since 1971, has yet been prepared. One of the accused continues to be a Senior Minister of the Government and the other is currently an ambassador. The public has lost confidence in the institution.

United Nations Human Rights Commission and International Labor Organization:

Much material has been made available to the United

Nations High Commission and the I L O to bring to their attention the considerable degree of racial discrimination prevailing in Guyana, and the situation was in fact discussed by the Commission at its annual session during February 1974 in New York. Results of their study of the problem are eagerly awaited.

The ILO has requested the government to rectify the Convention on Discrimination which it has so far refused to do, for obvious reasons.

General comment:

It could be seen from the above the extent of the economic, social and cultural genocide which is taking place among the majority of the East Indian population by a minority regime, and we call upon all peoples of the world will have been clamoring for an end to racial discrimination to raise their voices against the trend of events in Guyana before it is too late. The government of Guyana has so far been completely indifferent to all peaceful protests, and persists in its rule ruthless campaign of suppression.

The " there wishes to express its thanks to the D.C. I know for sending to the other parts of the Caribbean, this by able document concerning the present conditions under which or brothers and sisters of Guyana are present suffering.

BEST (NEGRO) VILLAGE

Over the last month radio, television and the press have bombarded us with a festival that claims to be national, but which is, in fact, as racial as apartheid. We are referring to the Prime Minister's Best Village Competition, which is openly racial in the sense that it means to keep out Indians from any serious role. We have the farce of a show that aims to bring out village culture, but which almost totally excludes Indians who comprise more than 50 % of the rural population.

And it is evidence of the racist thinking of the negro groups in the country, even the anti-government ones, that none of them have seen fit to point out the fact. Let us remember that 71 % of the Indians in this country live in villages, and that more Indians live in rural areas than any other ethnic group. It is the negroes who are an urban group.

Indians have a culture and it definitely does not include steelband, calypso, French and Spanish folk songs and dances, parang, limbo and a stream of blacks prancing and gyrating for their messiah Eric Williams. The rare Indian item was clearly not part of the whole scheme. The planning, the format, the prizes, in fact the whole tone of the competition was negro, so it could only have been the Best Negro Village Competition.

The results published in the Guardian of November 30th tell the story even more clearly. There were 14 individual prizes for performers, including 12 individuals and two groups. No

Indian names appeared and the two groups were a parang band and a Spanish dance group. Six were nominated for extra-mural courses, none of whom were Indians. Nine wee recommended for scholarships and grants. Of these only one Indian-sounding name – Rabathaly – appears. Of over 50 individuals and groups awarded prizes only one was identifiably Indian – the Krishna Dancers. And since Krishna has said that he prefers to teach Indian dance to negroes rather than to Indians, the less said about such a gharria-licking stooge, the better.

The name of the competition suggests that the village putting on the best show of its culture would win. But Indian villages like Debe and San Francique did not appear neither did the village of Caroni. We prefer not to believe that these villages had no culture to show, and feel instead that the plan of the Prime Minister, the Ministry of Culture and the PNM was to exercise cultural apartheid against Indians. The Europeans and Americans have shown that it is not necessary to put up a sign saying "No Blacks Wanted' to deliver the message. In this show the organizers did not say "No Indians Wanted" but the message was plain for all to see.

We must also wonder what is a village in these days. Is Central East Port of Spain a village, or Fyzabad or Point Fortin, or North-West Laventille? Our understanding of a village in Trinidad and Tobago is that of a distinctly rural or agricultural area, smaller than the city or borough like Arima, or towns like Sangre Grande and Siparia. Yet we see large industrial centers like Fyzabad and Point Fortin transformed into villages.

We understand the picture only when we see that any place which contains a PNM party group or a PNM controlled community center has become a village. Presumably these folks will be so happy to see themselves on television (boring the life of frustrated viewers) that they will vote PNM in the next election come what may.

Again we must emphasize that none of the black groups, so-called fighters for freedom, justice and racial equality, have seen or talked of the racial, anti-Indian aspects of "Best Village". This is another in the long list of their crimes of omission and blindness to our fate – and we shall make them pay the penalty of no Indian support. After three years of Best Village we can no longer excuse groups like Tapia, Democratic Action Congress, Union of Revolutionary Organisations, New Beginning and United National Independence Party.

The Black Power group, National Joint Action Committee (NJAC) has at last protested against the show. But their concern is only for themselves and what they see as a mockery of their 'African' Culture. This group, which has been beating the drum of Afro-Indian unity for so long, again show that their call is no more than a slogan.

As far as we are concerned the PNM obviously wants to continue its ANTI-Indian cultural policy pretending that negro culture is Trinidad culture. They call this cultural integration, but we call it surrender of our culture and rightly oppose it. We place full blame on the PNM for it – but we note that the rank and file of the negro population goes along with, or strongly supports this policy. And we make conclusions to suit.

The motives of the PNM towards their own blacks are no secret when we realize that basically Best Village is something happening after 1970, the year of the black revolt against the PNM.

As poet Derek Walcott commented "The cultural expression of the Black Power movement is a ghetto expression which is formulated in funk and soul." The people who nearly toppled the PNM had an aggressive town style based on American funk, soul, rock and African revivalism.

To stifle this trend and turn back the clock, the PNM appear to be forcing the folk culture of Best Village on the blacks and us. They are trying at once to deculturate us by showing another people's culture as national culture and to keep down the image of Afros, dashikis and funk.

Says Walcott "The folk expression promoted by the Ministry of Culture is a pastoral expression. It seems unreal to project a pastoral image of the folk asserting its African roots, when what one is principally confronting is an urban expression with the same roots."

Even Walcott, However, clear-sighted as far as the blacks are concerned, is blind to our problem. We are not folks until we assert our African roots, it would seem.

SHORT STORY

The Doolaha

By Miss Rajnie Ramlakhan

"Dat eh Siew passing on de road?"

"Yeah, is he self."

"I hear he getting married Sunday, I glad for him."

"Yes man, he is a good boy, very ambitious."

" I always say he get what he want. Doh min' he ent working no way, is only a minor setback."

Siew wanted to a burst out laughing. Only a few days ago he was a lazy good-for-nothing scam. He had no ambition. He would beg all the days of his life. Suddenly all that changed. He became the most talked-about person in the village.

Wives who would normally look away whenever he passed, stared him boldly in the eyes and smiled. Elders and husbands hailed out to him as if they were good friends. Children stood aside respectfully for him to pass. Young girls giggled and pointed at him. Young men patted him on the shoulders, with wicked smiles in their eyes. When a man was to be married in Gandhi Village, he was King.

For Siew, it started the day he went to "see" Sumintra, accompanied by his parents, a few relatives and a pundit. She was brought before him, head heavily veiled and resolutely bent.

Sumintra's father---"You like she son?"

Siew. . . . ---"How I....."

"Yes, I find she pretty, she go make a nice daughter-in-law," his mother interposed.

Siew's father---"Let Punditji read their patra first and see if they suitable."

So punditji commenced reading their 'patra' (horoscope). He stared intently at the palms. He leafed through his decaying books. He traced their fingers around pictures. He consulted more books. Then in a very solemn voice, he pronounced them compatible and marriageable.

Sumintra's father---"Well son, what you say, you go marry she?"

Siew---"But I still haven't . . ."

Siew's mother. . . "Yes he go married she Punditji, fix the date."

The date was fixed two months hence.

So his reign began as his marriage drew nearer.

Neighbor-"Siew, you fulling water and you wedding is Sunday? You mad? Ramesh, go fill up some water for Siew to bathe."

Aunt ...."Tara, iron a pants and shirt for Siew to put on."

Mother.... "Indra, you carry Siew food for him?"

Cousin..... "Gita, go and make up Siew bed."

Father...... "Why you lifting them heavy bamboo? Leave it, we will build the tent."

Siew, realizing the situation, capitalized on it. He ordered the children around. He swindled cigarettes and drinks out of the men. He lashed out against the elders "tyranny and domination ." He joked scandalously with the women and young girls. He smoked leisurely while the young men built the tent. He slept soundly when they filled the barrack.

Saturday night came, the night of his "cooking". Siew sat comfortably, arms folded, surveying the situation. The tent was buzzing with activities. Men were arranging tables and chairs; children washing wares and "soharee leaves"; women and girls peeling vegetables, kneading flour. Fires were being lit. In one corner some old women were entertaining everyone with their "wedding songs" and music. Siew smiled benevolently with everyone.

Around midnight, he yawned and stretched. Time to sleep, he thought. He expected everything would be ready by morning.

"You think Sumintra must be crying?", someone asked him. Sumintra? Then he remembered. He was going to marry her. All well, she would have to serve him loyally. She would have learnt from the experience.

Early the next morning, Siew was bathed and oiled, and carried into the tent. He sat centrally, surrounded by a sea of admiring faces belonging to colorfully dressed villagers. He was then robed in his magnificent "jama-jor, clothes befitting a King. The pundit placed the crown gingerly on his head. He could almost hear him say, amidst loud applause and ringing cheer, "I appoint you King of Gandhi Village."

He bowed graciously and acknowledged their joy. Then someone said "Your majesty, your royal couch awaits you."

He was lifted again and taken into the gaily bedecked car. He smiled with everyone, and with a royal wave, they were off. He was preceded by a car from which flowed royal music for his entire journey. He was followed by his usual retinue of supporters. He hoped that everything would be properly arranged on the other side.

The drive was a smooth, relaxing one. Now he was only two streets away from his destination. His heart began to beat just a little bit faster. He adjusted his crown, straightened out his clothes, looked in the mirror. He would do. His father, sitting next to him, nodded his satisfaction. The place was a bit quiet, thought Siew. He looked outside. No one was in sight, as was to be expected. Everybody would be at Sumintra's awaiting his arrival.

Then they reached the corner to turn into Sumintra's yard. The entire procession stopped and started again. They were going to make a grand entry. Siew's car slowly turned the corner and - no tent, no milling crowds, no welcoming party! Siew was puzzled. Did they have the wrong date, perhaps? He glanced at his father. He shrugged. They stopped in front of the house. Still no one came.

"Maybe somebody sick", said his father.

"Maybe", muttered Siew.

Everybody sat in their cars waiting, quietly, anxiously. The music was stopped. Siew was beginning to get answers. What was the delay all about? He looked outside. Over by the neighbor next door, some little boys were playing marble pitch, unconcerned. Maybe there had the wrong day. Why didn't someone come to them? Surely, Sumintra's parents must know they were outside.

Then, suddenly a tear-stricken, old woman emerged from the house.

"Sumintra run away!" she blurted out.

••

COMMENTARY

BLACK RACIST VISITS TRINIDAD

President Nyerere, black dictator of Tanzania, is currently visiting Trinidad. The President confessed to his hosts that he was surprised to see blacks so well-fed, and looking so well. He did not say anything about the starving Asians he saw. Nor did he say anything about rumours that he plans to kick out the well-fed Asians from Tanzania, or his failure to feed black Tanzanians.

P.S. The President has since denied rumours of the impending expulsion of Asians, but he was careful to distinguish between those Asians who are citizens of Tanzania and those who are British citizens. Readers will recall the ruse the skunk Amin used when he expelled all Asians. Nyerere noted *en passant* the real reason why he came to Trinidad. We have things Tanzania needs.

Indians in Belize

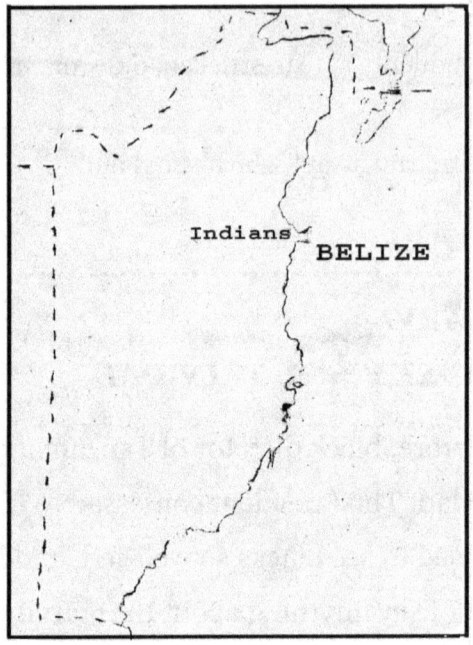

A British claim in Central America, carved out of the Spanish Conquistador stampede through the New World, Belize exists as an "insult" to the presence of the Latin American umbrella along the Caribbean seaboard of Central America. Also shipped to fill in the labour supply for plantations of sugar cane and citrus, were the children of India.

Latest reports indicate that these 5,000 or more Indians are cut off from the base of the Indian pyramid which comprises of Surinam, Guyana and Trinidad. Their major contact for their survival of Indian lifestyles, exists with the Indians of Jamaica, as they, the Indians in Belize, struggle to break through the social and economic barriers of plantation existence.

At the present time, they are making a breakthrough into shopkeeping, the lower ranks of the civil service and teaching. The more fortunate, who number the very few, have been able to enter the professions by access to university education. Here too, cut off from India and existing in the Belize society as a small, and depressed minority, deculturation has taken place.

Yet the Indians in Belize pride themselves on the Indianness which has survived, and are anxious to make contacts with other Indians in the Caribbean. Most of the Belize Indians still live in rural areas with their local leaders and carry out relationships for their day to day survival.

The Indians of Belize now send out the smile of friendship across the Caribbean to Indians in other countries in the chain that extends from Surinam on the Southeast to Belize in Northwest.

The State of Hindu Society

K. R. Lalla

To obtain a true picture of the present state of the Hindu society, it will be interesting to look somewhat briefly into our historical past. Hinduism is one of the oldest religions in the world. Radhakrishna in his book entitled *The Hindu View of Life* said:-

The dictum that, if we leave aside the blind forces of nature, nothing moves in this world which is not Greek in its origin, has become common place with us. But this is not altogether true. Half the world moves on independent foundations which Hinduism supplied – China and Japan, Tibet and Siam, Burma and Ceylon look to India as their spiritual base. Thee historic records date back to over four thousand years and even then it reached a stage of civilization. It has stood the stress and strain of more than four or five thousand years.

So ancient and established has been the Hindu religion that it has influenced not only the countries mentioned but even other countries such as Iran, Turkey, European countries and others too numerous to mention.

It is said that Iran brought Hindu thought to the Greek. It is further stated that it was in Iran that Pythagoras in the 6th century B.C. learnt his Hindu ideas in philosophy and mathematics. Moreover, there is evidence that Greek geometry borrowed from Sulba Sutras. Further that echoes of Hindu doctrines of Karma and rebirth are clear to Plato, the great Greek philosopher. Greek medicine was indebted to the Hindu Ajur Veda. Buddhist Jataka stories influenced the Christian gospels and parables in which over fifty parables have been pointed out.

W.K.Durant in his work entitled *Our Oriental Heritage* said: *Indeed India is probably responsible for most of the fables that have passed like an international currency across the frontiers of the world.* Indian astronomy and mathematics spread to the West and the Indian numerals, the invention of the zero and the decimal system are attributed to India by several histories of mathematics. The game of chess is yet another innovation of India in the world.

In the 19th century Trinidad and Tobago also became a beneficiary of the Hindu religion and culture.

It was on the 3rd day of May, 1845 that the famous ship named the *Fath Al Razack* arrived from Calcutta to the shores of Trinidad with 225 passengers. Their arrival here was due to the need for labour to save the complete collapse of the economy of this country. From the year 1845 the number of Hindus increased. They were transported from their homeland to a strange place. They came here as strangers to the conditions, social and otherwise. They were lumped into estates, where they lived in poverty and squalor.

There were no temples or places of worship. The language difficulty and the Western way of life imposed untold hardship on them.

The government of the day did not seem to care very much if at all about their educational and religious needs. It was at that juncture that the Canadian Mission came on the scene. The Canadian mission showed great interest in the educational needs of the Indians, but that was not without strings. The motivating factor of the Canadian mission was to convert the Indians to Christianity. In this connection the vast majority of Hindus were indeed adamant and therefore refused to be converted from Hinduism to Christianity. But there were others who through compulsion of one kind or another submitted to Christianity.

Those who resisted conversion were subjected to widespread discrimination and were denied educational and job opportunities. One Christian missionary wrote of the Hindus thus: *morally and spiritually they are as hard as stone and cold as an icicle.* Another Christian missionary reported that the more determined and resilient Hindus rejected the idea of conversion on the ground that *"we have a religion as well as you and cannot forsake it for a new one."* Donald Wood in his book entitled Trinidad in Transition said:

But the real difference between the Indian Immigrant and the others was a cultural one and not an administrative one. Concealed behind the term coolie with its derogatory undertones of ignorance and abject poverty were men in a social system which had only been touched superficially by three and a half centuries of European influence. Theirs was an intricate and subtle society which was fortified by...a religion, ancient when the Nestorian Christians had made their way to India and scarcely disturbed by post-Tricentine proselytizing since the days of St Francis Xavier and Nobili. If Africans were regarded as clay which could easily be molded into a Christian and Western shape, the Hindu of India were more like stone that could only be worked painfully with much toil. This was the reason, incidentally, why the Christian ministers in Trinidad looked at the influx of Indians with forebodings. Their pastoral work seemed to have become infinitely complicated by the aloof obstinacy of Hindus.

The present state of the Hindu society is nothing short of chaos and confusion; our Hindu brothers and sisters both young and old are disappointed, disillusioned and frustrated. We have on our hand a decaying society which is fraught with religious and social ills.

The all-important question that must be asked is who and what have contributed to the appalling state of our society.

Could we salvage our society from its present state of collapse?

It is now approximately 137 years since the arrival of fathers and forefathers from India and it is of great interest to reflect upon the fluctuating state of progress and deterioration from then until now.

When they came here they brought with them their language, customs, traditions and religion. The conditions under which they lived were indeed quite different from that which prevails today.

There were then no temples, nor any place of communal worship. As was customary in India, religious education and the conducting of religious services fell into the hands of the pundits. To meet the religious needs of the society, pundits visited the homes of individuals, who, from time to time so requested.

In the early days everyone spoke and understood Hindi, although not all were able to read and write the language. Pundits were, then as today, looked upon as the educated ones, and since they were in complete control of providing education and understanding of our religion. It was expected that efforts would have been made by them to establish proper methods of communicating with, and imparting knowledge of our religion to, the members of our society. Unfortunately, that was not so.

The system of visiting homes of individuals and conducting religious services meant that those who could not have afforded to invite pundits for that purpose had to do without any form of religious instruction or guidance. On the other hand people could not have a katha or Suruj Pooran every week or month; in most cases people could not have afforded to have any at all, while on the other hand there were those who could do so but occasionally.

Apart from this form of religious exposure, there were no other machinery established for educating and instructing our people in our religion with the disastrous result that most if not all our Hindu brothers and sisters today have little or no knowledge or understanding of the various aspects of our religion.

The gross neglect of the education and religious needs of our people must be placed fairly and squarely on our religious teachers and leaders. For, over a century and more, generations upon generations of our religious leaders and teachers have come from the same homes, caste and stock. This meant that the performance of religious ceremonies, and the control of the growth and development thereof were confined within the domain of the pundits. This monopoly has continued for over a century or more with little or no significant change in the institutional structure. In fact, what we have witnessed over the years is the deep division amongst our pundits and the sharp conflict and variation in the methods and procedures in conducting religious services.

The persistent rivalry and disunity amongst our religious leaders and teachers and their patent failure to bridge the widening gap of rivalry have produced a deleterious effect on the minds of our people.

Their failure to produce a uniform system or method of conducting religious services has left our people in a state of utter confusion. If you were to ask the vast majority of our young and even the old people to give some explanation of their understanding of some of our religious events such as *Kartik, Janamashmi, Shivratri, holi,* and *pitrapaksh* you will be astonished to learn how little they know about them. What is indeed very disturbing is that very often the explanation given by those who are supposed to know the aspects of our religion differs one from the other with the result that the widespread ignorance which already looms over the society, about the knowledge and understanding of the tenets of our religion is thereby compounded.

While our religious leaders and teachers have been content to uphold the time-honoured practice of conducting religious services from home to home, here today and there tomorrow, the religious leaders of other denominations were and have been busily engaged in planning and constructing churches, mosques and educational institutions, not only for the purpose of educating their followers in the principles and foundation of their religion, but also for the purpose of providing them with a formal education.

So that while the Hindus have been allowed to remain stupid and ignorant for the want of a proper and well-established medium for propagating and disseminating knowledge and understanding of our religion and culture, the other denominations have been forging ahead.

It is well-known that our religious leaders and teachers go to no theological school or institution for training and education. Whatever they have learnt has been taught to them by their parents. No efforts, however, have been made so far to provide such an institution. Because of their limited education, they have not been able to study and keep abreast with the changing patterns in our religious and cultural needs. Over the years, we have had visiting us from India, numerous missionaries, and one of the striking and noticeable features about them has been their high standard of education, not only in religion but also in other fields such as economics, law and sociology. Their knowledge of the Vedas and the Gita and the Ramayan and the host of other religious books have always created such a resounding impact on us that we have never failed to look forward to their return.

To become a Christian priest a person attends university or some theological institution before assuming the role of a religious teacher or leader. The Christian priest is trained, not only to take care of the religious needs of his parishioners, but is also sufficiently equipped to look into their social and educational needs as well. If a person of the Christian church needs a recommendation, he calls on his parish priest. If he needs any kind of guidance or assistance he calls on his parish priest. The same cannot be said about the Hindu society. In fact many of our Hindu brothers and sisters in time of real need are compelled to seek the assistance of Christian priests because the same type of services is not available to them through their own religion.

To quote a further illustration about the inadequacy of our religion, the Christian priests hold Sunday School in all their parishes and teach their young ones all about their religion so that when they grow up they would have a sound knowledge and understanding of their religion.

The question that must be asked is how many religious classes do we conduct in our society, and in how many areas? Christian and Muslim priests visit members of their religion in the hospitals, the prisons, the orphan homes and numerous other social institutions thereby providing them with faith, confidence and security in their religion. Hindus do not enjoy these privileges and as a consequence they feel lost, neglected and unwanted. Our brothers and sisters in such unfortunate circumstances feel dejected and conclude that the other religions and their leaders are indeed greater than and superior to ours.

A daily spectacle in our villages and districts where there is a preponderance of Hindus is the operation of numerous organizations busily engaged in converting our young boys and girls from Hinduism to other religions.

Some of you might say that the existence of such a state of affairs cannot be fully attributed to the apathy and indifference of our religious teachers and leaders but that the blame should be shared equally by parents. While this may be a reasonable conclusion, it must at the same time be borne in mind that parents can only give that which they have. How could we expect a parent to teach a child arithmetic when he knows nothing about arithmetic. It follows that parents who have themselves remained stupid and ignorant of their religion cannot be expected to give that which they do not have.

The daily conversion of our young boys and girls from Hinduism to Christianity has been a very troubling question, and is a matter which requires urgent and immediate attention, but to whom could we turn for this urgent and immediate attention? What has happened and continued to happen over a century and more is that our religious leaders and teachers have remained unconscious and pathetically unaware, either by design or through their own ignorance, of the rapid sociological changes which have been taking place in the Hindu society.

Today we no longer wear the same kind of clothes as our fathers and forefathers. The dhoti and kurta are only worn on special occasions and even so by a significant few. Our young girls do not wear *orhni* and *ghangari* and *jhula*. Hindi is no longer spoken in the home.

The Western culture and way of life have made and continue to make a tremendous impact on our mode of dress, food, language and habits. We have become so absorbed in the Western way of life without even realizing the extent and degree.

So that while gradually and without being fully conscious of the rapid erosion of our religion and heritage wrought by westernization, we are caught hustling and bustling without any plan, programme or research to protect what is left. While this social transmission is currently taking place, so too our religious and cultural and social values have been sinking.

On the question of leadership generally, it would be somewhat uncharitable to say that our past as well as our present leaders have failed us miserably. Looking at the past and comparing it with the present leads to the incontestable conclusion that all our leaders have conspired in one way or another to keep us in a state of perpetual ignorance and subjection.

The absence of responsible leadership has produced untold and disastrous consequences. The quality of leadership that we have witnessed over the years has been one fraught with dominance, and self-aggrandisement. There has always been the traditional hostility by one leader against another, or by one faction of leaders against another. We have witnessed rivalry upon rivalry, backed by connivance and collusion. The consequences of that caliber of leadership has produced a chronic state of fragmentation amongst us, with the attendant result of a high degree of frustration and disillusionment.

The widespread fragmentation and disillusionment have inflicted upon us a psychological and sociological inferiority complex which is indeed very pronounced in the personality make-up of our people.

Our women-folk have, by design, been relegated to a state of subjection and discrimination. Wile women in India and other parts of the world have become a vibrant and dynamic force, in our Hindu society our women have been the victims of discrimination and segregation. The treatment meted out to them has been a monstrous sociological problem. The suicide rate among our Hindu folk is very high and this can be attributed to frustration of one kind or another.

Our religion is one of the richest in yoga philosophy and wisdom. There are numerous books written about our religion, philosophy and culture, but alas, over the the period of 137 years we have not seen fit to establish a library or an archive for the purpose of accumulating and housing such books. It is not surprising, therefore, that our only source of knowledge is what we are told by others.

Over the past years court actions were instituted by our distinguished leaders for the purpose of settling their quarrels and petty differences. The filing of such court actions has not only added to the frustrations and disillusionment of the whole Hindu society, but has stupefied and stultified non-Hindus as well. Those actions have had the effect of holding the whole Hindu society to ransom. While resorting to court actions may have been regarded by those involved as the most reasonable method of approach towards settling their disagreement, to the vast majority of us it has been considered to be most undesirable and degrading. While court actions were pending determination those who suffered and continue to suffer were not the litigants themselves, but the vast majority of our innocent Hindu brothers and sisters.

There are other religious denominations in our country as I have pointed out hitherto, but it can hardly be said that they have pursued court actions as the medium through which they sought to settle their differences.

One may therefore ask the question on how many occasions have the leaders of the Catholic Church resorted to court actions to settle their internal disputes; on how many occasions have the leaders of the Anglicans, the Methodists, the Presbyterians etc instituted court actions to resolve domestic quarrels?

Is it that the leaders of all these organizations are endowed with a higher degree of intelligence and wisdom than our leaders? Or is it that the leaders of these denominations are possessed pf higher spiritual values and a greater sense of dedication towards the common good and general welfare of their people? These are indeed questions that require study.

The fragmentation of our society has resulted in the mushrooming of organizations upon organizations throughout the country.

What we have been witnessing, therefore, over the years, is the emergence of a multiplicity of leaders and fly-by-night organizations coming into existence with all the trappings and fanfare, but soon go out of existence, most unceremoniously. The emergence of these organisations, however, establishes that there are people in our society who are deeply concerned over its disorganized, fragmented and appalling state and are indeed anxious and enthusiastic to make some contribution to its deteriorating state, but alas, they themselves operate without a plan, programme or research.

The Hindu society today can boast of having a large number of professionals qualified in almost every field. We have doctors, lawyers, engineers, economists, sociologists, historians, accountants, teachers, political scientists and a host of others. Yet the cry for leadership goes unheard. Why do the vast majority of these professionals shy away from our Hindu society? You may or may not agree with the statement that the more qualified the Hindu, the less he wishes to be identified with his religion: and this is more applicable to our young girls.

If our society is to be saved, then the time to act is now. It is of fundamental importance to embark upon a study of the numerous factors which have been working havoc over us. In this connection what must be done now, without further procrastination, is to set up a Research Council to study and analyze the different areas of weakness in our society and to make such recommendations as circumstances require.

There is dire need for true and enlightened leadership

The qualities and characteristics of true and genuine leadership are that the individual must possess a good and sound education; discipline, strength of character and integrity, reliability and a sense of justice and fairplay, and the ability to persevere and overcome discouragement when things go wrong; he must possess a sense of goodwill, selflessness and humility.

These qualities and qualifications set a very high standard, but they are indeed essential in any leader. If we have failed in the past it is only because our leaders have lacked the qualities and characteristics of good leadership.

Nehru said of Gandhi and Tagore:

No two persons could be so different from each other in their makeup or temperament. But they seemed to represent different but harmonious aspects of India and to complement one another. Both of them, though vastly different and yet so alike. Nothing stood between these two great men when it came to work for the people, although they represented two extremes.

What our society needs now more than ever is a blood transfusion. It seems that the old blood has grown weak and infective and needs replacing by new blood.

But this transfusion is now taking place in many areas; in fact it has already taken place in Prices Town. The symbol of this transfusion is this beautiful and magnificent Mandir. This

Mandir is indeed the symbol of the unity of thinking of the members of the Sanatan Seva Sangh. This Mandir represents hard work, cooperation and faith in our religion. It has come after a century or more, but it has nevertheless come at a crucial time in our history.

This Mandir has re-kindled the pride and dignity in our religion which has been fast disappearing.

The organization of this seminar is yet another milestone in the list of achievements of the officers and members of the Sanatan Seva Sangh.

This may well be the beginning of a new era in the history of our society. It is certainly the turning of a new page in the history of our society.

It is my fervent wish and hope that this new blood transfusion will continue to take place with speed and rapidity.

Indians in Jamaica

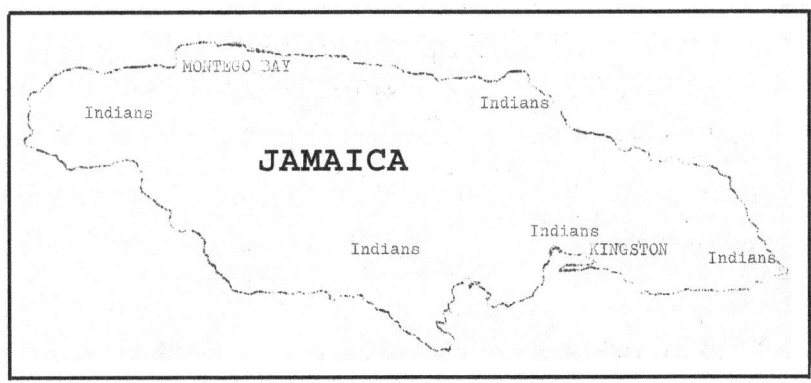

Arising out of a shortage of labour in the West Indies in 1844, the British House of Commons passed an act which resulted in the following.....

From 1845 through 1916, approximately 30,000 indentured labourers from India arrived in Jamaica, bringing with them Indian culture to a new land which was to become for many, a new homeland. The culture they brought with them, was that of a peasant way of life, at the centre of which was the Indian mode of life (Dharma).

Dharma has a religious basis embodying a philosophy of life and a code of ethics, emphasizing service, dedication and effort on the part of every individual, towards greater harmony within himself, with his immediate environment, and indeed the whole universe.

The Indians, mostly Hindus, the rest Muslims, came to Jamaica as a humble people in a strange land, not being able to speak English, and the great majority being unable to read and write in their native languages, though their ability to express their own ideas in their spoken tongue was excellent. However, there were a few, especially those belonging to the Brahmins, who could read and write Sanskrit, the root of the Indian languages, as well as Hindi or another language, depending on what part of India they came from. (The Muslim priests read Urdu or Arabic.)

At first the migrants lived on the estates in close-knit villages and their life style was a blend between their traditional customs and a typical Jamaican way of life. They were concentrated in the sugar belts and banana producing areas. Thus they could be found at George's Plain and surrounding areas in Westmoreland, Holland in St. Elizabeth, Vere Plains of Clarendon, various areas in St Mary, and to a lesser degree in Portland, St. Thomas and St. Catherine. Many stayed in Kingston and mainly planted vegetables.

The cultural practices of this ethnic group was centred around the priests (Pundits) among the Hindus and the Mulvis among the Muslims, who were considered leaders. The priest would conduct ceremonies. Give advice, settle disputes and in some cases, attend to sickness. In return, he received honour from the people, gifts of food, as well as pay for consultation over superstitious matters. On the whole the priests were good men, many remaining vegetarians and living disciplined lives. But as far as the propagation of the culture is concerned, they largely failed to pass on their knowledge to younger ones..

Among Hindus the main fault of the priests was petty rivalry among themselves and their attitude of propagating remnants of a "Caste" system which is unsuitable to the needs of a modern changing world. Most were not fluent at English and failed to explain the significance of the tradition they fostered to the younger generation, the majority of whom knew little of the Indian languages. They also remained out of touch with India and the changes that were taking place in the Motherland, so that their practices remained stagnant and in some cases, outdated. Many of the younger generation became Christians.

Some of the Hindu ceremonies performed by the priests and which are still being done to a lesser extent today, are Pujas and Kathas, and Moorans (commemorating the cutting of a child's hair), Festivals observed are Divali (Festival of lights) between October and November, and Phagwah or Holi between February and March. Muslim religious services include Maulood Sharif and Kuran Sharif, while Festivals observed are Nurnama Ramadan and Eid-ul-Fitr. The well-known and colourful "Hussay" of the Muslims also had a religious background and is celebrated.

Generally, the decline in the numerical strength of the priests in Jamaica coincides with the decline in the cultural practices of Indian origin. Indeed in our present day many young people, especially in the rural areas, have never attended an "Indian Function", and of those who have had the opportunity to do so, few understand the background to what is carried on.

Today, there are only two mulvis and three pandits in the entire Jamaica and the scope for Indian culture and religious practices centred around are very limited.

At present there are three organizations which at present serve to direct and assist in the survival of Indian culture in Jamaica. They are the East Indian Progressive Society, which was founded in 1940; the Sanatan Dharma Mandir formed in 1965 which is in the process of constructing a temple and fosters Hinduism; and the Prema Satsangh Friendly Society which was founded in 1972 and pursues religious, cultural and social activities.

Indian recipes
(A defense of Indian cooking)

At the present time when the whole educational system in the Caribbean has been and continues to be designed to erase all Indian-ness and knowledge of an Indian lifestyle, the preparation of food is no exception.

When one sees that the Indian girl in the secondary school is being compelled by her teacher who is totally ignorant of the value and necessity of Indian cookery or scorns her own past after self-contempt has been instilled into her mind, the individual becomes angry at the perpetration of such brutality on the Indian society.

The Indian girl is becoming alienated from her own food, in the learning process of the school, and the emphasis on western foods makes Indian cookery either something to be ashamed of, or what which must be forgotten. This absurdity reaches its zenith in the university graduates, the bank clerks and the civil servant who talk of curry they have been eating all their lives as 'exotic Indian dishes'.

Serious misconceptions and the propaganda of lies are at present being circulated in informal comments of conversations..... that Indian food 'does give run-belly', that 'kharhee' does give 'shittings'. One finds that the Indian elite finds it insultive when a rural friend of Caroni or Barrackpore, talks of eating 'roti and dasheen-bush bhagee'. This is the so-called self-appointed 'modern Indians', who grew up on bygan choka and sadha roti,now voice their derisive comments on how they hate 'coolie food', as they stuff themselves with 'french fries'... fry aloo, and boast of the dry-cardboard-tasting turkey they enjoy.

The individual can turn his or her memory back to the Christmas greetings of the Canadian based Indian students who tell mamoo and ahjee to 'save a piece of the turkey' (they never ate at home) for them. No different is the Indian girl who scorns to put her cutex-fingernails in dough, or finds it troublesome to make the low-yah, while she is a glutton for the sidewalk roti.

It is our consciousness of this brain-washing process into which Indians have been subjected, that makes them into "monkeys .. striving for evolution" into the dominating culture of Europe, and lately pseudo-Africanism, which causes the Indian elite to behave in such a ridiculous manner.

The deceitful dualism in them is displayed in their mid-week sermons of disgust for Indian food, as they speak to other Indians and non-Indians in their office- breaks and party-gaiety, while they hurry to that Sunday cook at the rural relative to stuff their hungry bellies with all the massala and dosti that mousie is proud to cook for her Port-of Spain and San Fernando nephews and nieces.

Indian cookery in the Caribbean, now branded under the dog-tag of West Indian cookery, is really an off-shoot of the cooking of Uttar Pradesh, Calcutta and Madras. The development and growth of Indian cookery coincides with the survival of the

Indian civilisation that spans Some five thousand years of unbroken history. And for these many years, Indian cookery has been passed on from generation to generation in the "mother teaching, laughter learning" process where information and actual skills are passed on to future wives and daughters.

However this process of cultural transmission has been seriously affected by mother-in-law,daughter-in-law relationships of the immediate past, and at present time, daughters succumb to school-mis-education that teaches them to disregard or scorn Indian cooking , so much so that they complain that Indian food is difficult to make while they spend hours learning how to make 'French souffles' and the 'chow ming' that turns out to be vegetables fried as bhagee.

The process of passing on the recipes has been subject to inadvertent alteration, in attention to details, short-cut methods, unavailability of certain items and the lapse of certain customs which required the preparation of special dishes. One sees this most conspicuously in Indian Presbyterianised homes of Princes Town that strive to make burnt-sugar-tasting Christmas-fruit cakes, the S.A.G.H.S. Moslem teenager with her 'Yorkshire pudding', and the Couva-convent-Hindu with her beef pies. Conveniently or deliberately forgotten are the adding bhagee leaves to dhal and the use of dahi which are beneficial for health purposes, while other 'customs' can add greater flavour to side dishes.

In this column, we shall attempt to give not only recipes, but also remind readers of the more useful 'old fashioned' Indian cooking customs. There is no need to be ashamed of the word 'old fashioned' as many of our young people are taught to believe. 'Old fashioned', in merely a phrase that refers to a period of time, and we too will not like to conceive ourselves as being old fashioned ten or twenty years from today.

Yet, in the day to day modern living of the secondary school, while Indian food is being disregarded and scorned by the propagators of 'white' culture, it is the perceptive eye of the researchers in Food Technology at the University of the West Indies, who have given public praise to the valuable nature of Indian cooking customs, which the ANTI-Indian mass media of press, radio and television have censored from their news broadcasts and publications.

Because of the way in which Indian cooking developed has developed here, and since we are aware of the variety of ways in which many dishes are prepared in different households, we would welcome any alternative recipe which is different, in method of preparation or food content, to that which is published here.

Since we are aware that Indian women do pride themselves on their expertise in Indian cooking, we wish that you share some of this valuable knowledge with our readers. We therefore welcome your suggestions for both recipes and cooking tops for publication from all our readers.

FLOUR BARFI ..... also called PAYRA

Ingredients

1 pound flour pound

1 pound sugar

1 tin condensed milk

8 grains elichee (also ca11ed cardamom)

2 ounces ghee (or three level teaspoons)

3 cups cooking oil

Method

Knead the flour with water unti1 fairly smooth. Divide the dough into halves. Roll out one half onto a floured chowkee (board) until thin. Cut into strips 1 inch wide and then immerse in 1/2 cup oil and stretch with fingers until dough is as thin as possible. It does not matter if the dough breaks while this is being done. Repeat with other half of dough.

You should now have a heap of thin strips of dough which you must now fry in the rest of the oil. This oil should be smoking hot and the dough must be left in the pot for only a very short time, so that, while crisp, it does not become brown.

Mince the fried strips finely into a white powder which must be dried in the sun for about an hour (or in a warm oven. Then place the sugar in the pot with enough water to dissolve it and add the elichee seeds which have been removed from their husks and thoroughly pounded so that they are cracked and their flavour is released into the syrup. Boil this syrup until it is very thick and begins to crystallise. Then pour this into the white flour powder to which the condensed milk and ghee has already been added.

Mix very quickly and then turn into a greased tray.

Leave as long as possible before cutting into rectangular blocks.

....

COMMENTARY

FIVE INDIANS GET AWARDS

A grand total of five Indians received awards in the Independence Day National Awards list. A total of 44 blacks, including off-blacks, received awards. We take this to mean:

1) Indians are a small minority of the population, perhaps 10 % and that they might even be "a hostile and recalcitrant minority."

2) That Indians are by nature *dishonorable* and are not worthy of national *honours.*

3) That Indians might melt the gold, silver and brass and ship it to India.

Indians in St. Lucia

ST. LUCIA

The Indian population is concentrated in four main areas; Vieux Fort, Ojiere, Forestiere, and Maraca. Indians comprise some 5% of the island's population and number about 6,000. According to my informant, few Indians are well off, the majority being poor. The society, however, does not make a distinction between rich and poor Indians. Both face the same in justice, the same pressures. Of the few Indians who succeeded in business, they were "forced" to marry their children to negroes. This is the price of success.

Racial chauvinism is just part of the general hostility towards Indians in Lucia. The blacks feel that everyone should intermarry and "form one race". Everything Indian has been suppressed. The Indians could not even listen to the Indian radio programs from Trinidad and Guyana in their own homes. It was difficult to understand why there should be this hostility and racialism since Indians do not constitute an economic, social or political threat to the blacks.

There still seem to be Indians who know something about Indian cookery. I met an Indian waitress in Castries who explained that roti sold in Castries was made by the Chinese and was unlike the Indian roti, which she could make, having learned from her mother.

The Indians in St. Lucia used to have Indian parties at which Indian food was served, and there was Indian singing and the recitation of the Ramayana by the older generation. The last such party took place about two years ago.

There seems to be some survival of Hindi among the older Indians. The Indians have been more fortunate, to the extent that a great many names have survived the onslaught of converting the Indians and changing their names.

It is felt that Indians should organize themselves into a department which would function as a trade union, and which would fight for the rights of all the Indians, participate in discussions at a national level, and propagate Indian culture. It appears that the Indians are afraid to follow the religions of their ancestors, because they may face greater religious and social discrimination.

The Indians a very conscious of their problems and their interests It is also reported that there may be unfavorable reactions to any Indian organization that decides to fight for the rights of all Indians, and as such, a great deal of caution is necessary. The the Indians are in need of books on Hindi, Indian culture, history and Indian records. They are also in need of people who can teach them more about their own Indian cultural expressions, dance and music. It is also necessary for others to go to these places and be able to obtain a better evaluation of the needs of the Indians and their problems.

....

COMMENTARY

THE LOST HINDUS

I sometimes think that anthropology is the undertaker of the social sciences, if only because of its necessary assumption of stasis. Take this man Dan Crowley, speaking of "lost Hindus." In what way are Hindus lost? Crowley seems to have missed the continuous contact we have always had with India, which has more or less kept us in the mainstream of Hinduism. The only lost Indians we know are those in St. Vincent, whose identity seems to have been hidden by colonial census officers. But Mukdar is busy tracing them, and we shall keep readers informed. Meanwhile we might find space to write about lost anthropologists.

to the west-INDIAN

By Krishna Ganeesingh

reach forward with your hands and mould your dreams
into reality, changing its shape in accordance with the
essential truths you carry in your being

walk in those footsteps where none has gone before, and
with your courage go towards the hopes you have silently
cherished

look to the distance that lies beyond the limited horizon
of your vision and let your imagination take you beyond
the limits imposed by your thinking

capture truth in the changing world around you, for
its beauty is a transient glimpse into the meaning of
life

drown all your uncertainties in the ocean of humility

and be yourself even when the world looks at you with
disfavour

and then will you find peace with the clamour of your yearning
for in that alone lies the contentment of your bliss.

INDIAN CULTURE AND CARIBBEAN POLITICS

Dr Balwant Singh

Probably as good as any of the numerous definitions of the subject is that "culture is what is left after everything we have learned has been forgotten. It consists of a deepened understanding, a breadth of outlook, an unbiased approach and a heart that has deep sympathy and strength of courage."

Culture dictates the way of life of a people, their response to given situations and their moral and ethnic values. A people without a culture is like a nation without an emblem.

The Caribbean for reasons of its history, is not only multiracial, but also a multicultural society adding thereby another facet to an image, the variety of which makes life generally so refreshing and so stimulating.

One of the important segments of this diversified culture is "Indian Culture," which is a living reality to over a million inhabitants of the Southern Caribbean area, the largest concentration of 500,000 being in Trinidad, followed by Guyana with 400,000 and Surinam 200,000.

One of the remarkable phenomenon of the history of the area is the extent to which the descendants of the immigrants from India have preserved whole parts of the culture which originally accompanied their ancestors, and which by regular cultural intercourse with India, through films, records, visiting troupes etc. has kept abreast of changes there.

Be he Hindu, Muslim or Christian, the Indian brought with him, not only the *Ramayana*, the *Gita*, the *Koran* and the *Bible*, but something which was common to them all.

And that something provided the impetus not only for survival but for prosperity. Some of the ingredients were a willingness to work hard, pray intently, save a little and keep the family unit together.

The Indians have music and most of this music is inspired by religion. The Hindus gather in Satsanghs (groups) and sing their bhajans (devotional songs) or chant the Ramayana while the Muslims sing their holy ghazals, often of their own composition, and meet in groups at melaub Shareef functions where holy renditions are done.

As with music, so with dance. The Indians have a tremendous love for dancing and most boys and girls at some stage try their hand at it.

The Indian immigrants also brought with them several languages – Hindi, Urdu, Arabic and to a lesser extent Tamil. And they contributed extensively to Caribbean diets with their curries, roti, pilau and the numerous varieties of sweet and salt delicacies – mitthai, pulorie etc.

It is true to say that the British colonialists, even though, by and large, did very little to actively support and encourage Indian culture in Guyana and Trinidad, did nothing to destroy it.

On the other hand, in Surinam, the Dutch rulers proved to be a great deal more generous towards it, and, for this reason

Hindustani (a mixture of Hindi of the Hindus and Urdu of the Muslims) is today a living language in that country, spoken by Indians as well as non-Indians, and Indian cultural institutions flourish there.

Unfortunately in Guyana today while the banner of cultural integration is being waved, the Indians find it difficult to escape the feeling that efforts are being made to distort if not destroy their culture. Even though they comprise 53 per cent of the population, they point out, that for instance the Government's cultural agency, the National History and Arts Council, has a rather low level of Indo-Guyanese content – 15 per cent and no allocation from its annual budget of G$500,000 is earmarked for the development of Indian culture.

It is also true to say that national institutions and facilities are not being made available for Indian cultural functions as post-independence experiences have shown. And the controversy relating to Indian and Afro=Caribbean culture could not even have been ignored during the staging of the historic 1972 Caribbean Festival of Creative Arts CARIFESTA). One of the reasons for the "Boycott Carifesta" call by Indo-Guyanese religious and cultural organizations was the absence of any of their representatives on the CARFESTA planning committee.

Trinidad and Surinam Indians are a great deal more fortunate with respect to cultural development generally, but it is obvious that there is still room for improvement. Surinamers are particularly proud that one of their four radio stations is devoted entirely to Indian cultural programmes.

The worry of the Indians about their culture naturally affect them economically. The Indian is predominantly a rural person and loves nature. He enjoys tending to his fields and his animals.

It is not surprising therefore that he has been deeply involved in the rice, sugar and cattle industries of the English-speaking Caribbean. But there is no need now to document the Indian contribution to agricultural development in the region.

It is sometimes claimed that fostering of Indian culture would be a divisive force in the Caribbean and this would ultimately lead to racial animosity. It must be remembered in this connection that a great deal of racial feeling is inspired by individuals who see racial cleavage as a vehicle for survival in public affairs, and culture is merely used as a scapegoat.

A distinguished writer in a comment on culture once said, "The problem of unity and diversity in culture is of interest to many people. Whereas, for instance, anthropologists want to analyze and interpret the cultural pattern of a people, the politician wants to change it. The politician's desire to change existing cultural patterns must, however, be distinguished from his ability to do so. The culture of a people is the product of centuries of adaptation to its environment and has a strength and resistance of its own.

Many multicultural societies in a haste to achieve national integration see culture as an obstacle to national unity and set about establishing mono-culturalism, but this only exacerbates the problem, as many perceive such a move as a threat to their "identity."

Clearly recognizable in the Caribbean are two main streams of culture – the Indian and the Afro-Caribbean, that admixture of nature and European culture.

The government of Guyana, for instance, is trying to revive the Amerindian dialects and to ascertain how best they could be made written languages. Would it not also be worth the effort, with far less expenditure, to foster the study of Hindustani, already a spoken and written language?

In conclusion I should like to say that the more than one million people of Indian descent who comprise about 25 percent of the total English-speaking Caribbean are part of the Caribbean. They know no other home and they recognize no other loyalties.

Their cultural practices should not be interpreted as an indication of separateness or an unwillingness to integrate. Cultural uniformity should not be the only criterion on which to base political loyalties.

Rather the diverse cultural pattern of the Caribbean arising out of the contribution of the various peoples who comprise its multicultural society, should be a source of strength and richness to the area.

On the other hand, if Indian culture is left on the periphery and not brought into the general stream of national development, it would continue to grow on the outside, and in time may really become a divisive force.

Politicians of the Caribbean clamour for regional

integration but the masses of the people do not seem to be part of the process. To what is then a basically fragile base, must be added the concern and fear of the Indo-Caribbean world.

Culturally, Indians see a desire among Southern Caribbean Politicians to "creolise" them by extinguishing completely the cultural flame which they have nurtured for about 140 years in these parts and which has provided them with the necessary energy.

Before regional integration could become a realistic proposition, politicians must allow the Indians full cultural freedom and not by their decisions and actions drive them into a corner to set up walls of resistance in defense of their cultural heritage, for these could very well become walls of separation.

It is my view, in light of what has been said before, that both streams should be actively encouraged and allowed to flourish separately, for they mean so much to the basic existence of the two major ethnic groups of the English-speaking Caribbean.

One certainly gets the impression that in the headlong drive for cultural integration both groups suffer from a feeling of suffocation and are denied freedom to expand and to give full expression to their desires. This explains to a large extent the cultural stagnation which prevails.

It is inevitable that evolution will take place and in the course of time subtle blending of both streams must occur resulting in what may be termed a truly Caribbean culture. In fact that is already happening with respect to diet, folk usages etc.

In the meantime there should be a positive effort to understand each other's cultural pattern and to preserve what now exists in order to add further to the richness of the society. Non-Indians should make a determined effort to understand the cultural background of the Indian and vice-versa.

While, for example Hindustani is a virile language in Surinam, it is a dying language in Trinidad and Guyana. This language is still being spoken or understood by a large portion of the Indian population of the Caribbean and is in fact the second language of the English-speaking Caribbean. It is the language of Hinduism and Islam and Indian culture.

Wouldn't the Caribbean be a much nicer place with Hindustani adding to the fragrance of its multi-coloured garden?

....

COMMENTARY: CHARITY BEGINS...ABROAD

It is strange now often the press reflects the folly and asininity of the society. It is no accident that the Guardian, being the country's biggest newspaper, is the most asinine. In an editorial of 22/09/1974 this newspaper openly called for aid for Belize and Honduras. Subsequent investigations have shown that *Alma* inflicted more damage in Trinidad than *Fifi* inflicted on Belize. Yet, nobody came to our aid. The government still has to implement a programme of aid for *Alma* victims. It cannot help its own people yet it is anxious to help others. Or is it that the government is unwilling to help Indians, who are the people who suffered the most damage?

85

Indians in Martinique

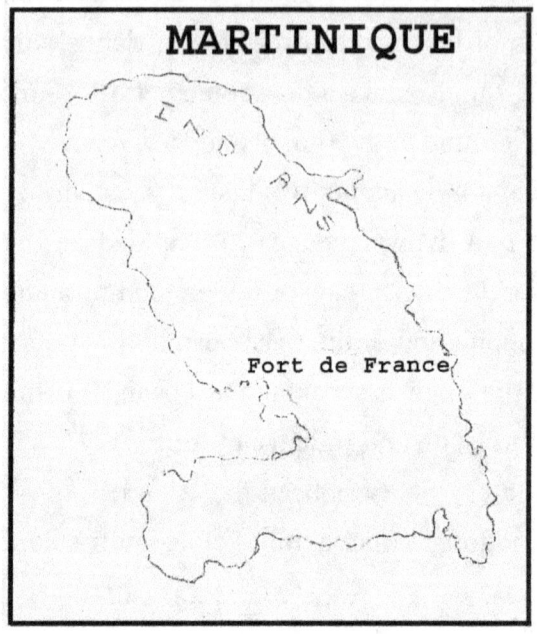

The Indians in Martinique have been as unfortunate as the Indians in the other islands of the Caribbean as Jamaica, St. Vincent and St. Lucia. Imported from India by the French colonials, to provide labour on the sugar plantations of Martinique. after the abolition of African slavery in the French West Indies, about 70,000 of them were shipped from the French Indian colonies.

Vidia Naipaul, in his book 'Middle Passage' page 204, writes of his 'discovery of the Indians of Martinique'. Naipaul writes,'I had never known there were Indians in Martinique... I had never known indentured Indians.... had replaced slave labour after emancipation, and that seventy thousand or more Indians had come to Martinique.'

The 'history' of the Indians of Martinique has been captured by Naipaul...'as one Martiniquan said to me with disgust and pride "They died like flies" '. This, no doubt, was the result of their exploitation by the French (Christian) planters. Under the crippling oppression in Martinique, they have been unable to escape the plantation and set up their own small farms by the purchase of land.

Because of this environmental factor in which the Indian has been unable to find land to purchase, in order to establish peasant farms, establish his own villages as was done by the Indians in Surinam, Guyana and Trinidad, he remains trapped in the barrack-life of dehumanised existence, where deculturation is rampant.

Yet Horowitz writes..."Martinique East Indians have maintained a complex and vigorous religion which thrives despite active discouragement of the Roman Catholic Church". They have established seven temples in Martinique, and are mainly located in the northern sugar lowlands of the island.

Naipaul writes of a conversation with the priest of the Hindu chapel. "He said he would have been able to keep up his 'Indian' if only he had someone he could practice it with".

Hindi – Who needs it?

It is obvious to all who want to see that an Indian revival is upon us and that nothing can stop it. One of the problems being faced in this revival is the question of language – and more specifically, the question of Hindi. What importance should be paid to speaking, writing, reading, singing and teaching in Hindi?

To answer, let us look at the culture being revived, the people doing it and their reasons. It is partly a religious revival, involving Hinduism, Islam, Buddhism, Jainism etc. and partly a cultural revival, which means looking again at the way of life and heritage of the Indians who came to Trinidad. We must not confuse the two and feel this is a Hindu revival. It is not. Christian Indians, Moslems, atheists are all interested.

Indian culture and religious practices were conducted in another language to the one we now speak, when our ancestors came here. English is our spoken language today, and it will remain so. Despite all efforts I see no other language becoming more than a second language to us.

A revival, crusade, or mass movement must be conducted in the language of the people, their spoken language or it will fail. Things only become meaningful to people when they understand the content. If the early Presbyterian missionaries had given their message in English instead of in Hindi they would have simply gained no converts. The idea is simple – communicate with people in the way they understand.

Now what is to be learnt and why? Culturally people want to know Indian history, their Indian past, Indian customs, songs, dances, philosophy, ideas, ways of thinking. They want to read works by Indian writers, see paintings. In short, they want knowledge of their Indian heritage, the value of which is now becoming plain to some of them.

Talks will be given, as well as lecture-demonstrations; books and pamphlets distributed, messages printed on T-shirts, buttons, posters. And naturally, the language for this sort of thing will be English. There is no disputing that the cultural revival, which is mainly the spreading of knowledge, has to be done in English.

Hindi cannot be used simply because enough people do not understand it, and to insist would stifle the message. It is vital that people learn, and to set conditions before allowing people to learn, is just suicide.

Besides, Hindi is only one language in India, and we are talking about an Indian cultural and religious revival including all India, but specially the provinces from where our ancestors came. There are at least 16 major languages in India and even there English is a common language, a common ground for the major languages. So why not use English here? To the people who are insisting that we learn Hindi we can ask why not Urdu, Tamil or Bengali for that matter? Must we learn Bengali to appreciate Rabindranath Tagore? So, we will read him in English like everybody else.

Though most of the Indians here are Hindus we must not

give the revival a Hindu flavour – it is an Indian revival. It would only be too easy for some people to drive even further the wedge between Hindus and Moslems. Hindi is particularly important to Hinduism, a matter we shall discuss in a while, but let us remember Arabic is no less important to Moslems and they do not let it choke them.

Hindi becomes quite important as far as the Hindu aspect of the religious revival is concerned, but even here it must have a smaller role than it does now, or else the same stifling will result. Prayers, songs, religious works, rituals are normally in Hindi or Sanskrit as they have been for the longest while. And the complaint is that because people do not understand Hindi they do not know the meaning of Hinduism – so they leave it for religions they can understand.

Is it necessary to know Hindi to be a Hindu? I feel it is useful, but not vital for the ordinary, and necessary for the pundits. To compare, Moslems are good Moslems, while many of them know less than a few words of Arabic or none at all. They are good Moslems because they understand Islam and practice it. The imams know Arabic, and use it for specified things, but they conduct their maktab or education classes in English. What is wrong with doing a similar programme for Hindus?

Hindi should not be wiped out totally and replaced with English but its place must be a definite and limited one. Some of the prayers and rituals could still be said in Hindi or Sanskrit, but even these must be explained in English. Nothing must be said or done that people do not understand. Ignorance of their religion by Hindu children has led to lack of interest and then conversion – the lesson has to be learnt.

Anything that has to do with instruction or education in Hinduism must be done in English. There are excellent translations or books in English and new ones, written by locals for our conditions must be written.

We must not bulge from this point – education must be done in the language of the people. Hinduism has survived because of its flexibility, not its stiffness. Even in India Hinduism is carried on, in all the languages, not exclusively in Hindu. It is the message that is important, not the dross of the messenger.

Many non-Hindus want to learn what is of value from India in the religious field. Even some Christian Indians are curious about the Gita and the Ramayan – but they are not going to learn Hindi to read them. As the other churches do, Hindus must see that all Hindu homes contain copies of the Holy Books that people can read easily. It takes a long time before anyone can learn enough Hindi to read the Gita.

People should be encouraged to learn Hindi, but we must realize that only a small percentage will become able to speak, write or understand it properly. Ability in Hindi must not be a passport for the ordinary man or he will go nowhere at all. Pundits and religious instructors must know it, so they can understand the meanings of the original language – and explain to the rest of us in English. Otherwise we read for ourselves what is not too complex, what translates well into English.

Let us realize that Hindi is not easily learnt, as it involves a new script, a new way of writing as well as a new vocabulary. Our children go to school for five years and study Spanish and French every day, but how many of them are able to make their way in those languages after a few years? How much Hindi will be learnt by people who are busily hustling for food, clothes and shelter? What everyone can learn in another language are some songs, rituals, greetings and so on.

Having the songs and prayers in English presents a problem, as people rightly say that in Hindi or Sanskrit or Arabic they create a special atmosphere and give a feeling that is lost in translation. That is true, and they should, some of them at least stay in the original language – as long as we know what they mean. We must no longer have to hang our head in shame when asked the meaning of the song or prayer we like so much. It is like the law: ignorance is no excuse. I expect lots of protests to these views on Hindi, saying much will be lost if English becomes prevalent. I reply that all will be lost if we continue as we are going – and I suspect that what they know will be lost is their position of importance, based on their knowledge of Hindi.

I suspect that man of the frauds who pose as experts on Hinduism just because they can read the Ramayan in Hindi will not be pleased. When everyone can read for themselves in English the true ignorance of some of these scoundrels will be exposed, so they stubbornly want to hold on to Hindi as a qualification for being Hindu or even for being Indian. They have used the people's ignorance of Hindi to advantage, knowing that hardly anyone could contradict them. All this must end.

The people must know the meaning of all they believe and practice, so they can correct the so-called leaders who have misled them. Hinduism, like the Indian way of life, has deteriorated simply because of the lack of knowledge by people, particularly the children. Islam has been luckier and better organized, but when the Indian way of life, which is carried on the shoulders of Hindus, so too do the Moslems, who share that way of living and thinking.

We must never let this happen again, for now Hindi must become a tool in our hands instead of a blindfold over our eyes.

....

COMMENTARY

ET ERGO IN ARCADIA

Reports from Northern Ireland state that mixed marriages "are the objects of hatred, ridicule, scorn and sometimes murder." "Mixed" here has nothing to do with race but refer to religion.

Indians in St. Vincent

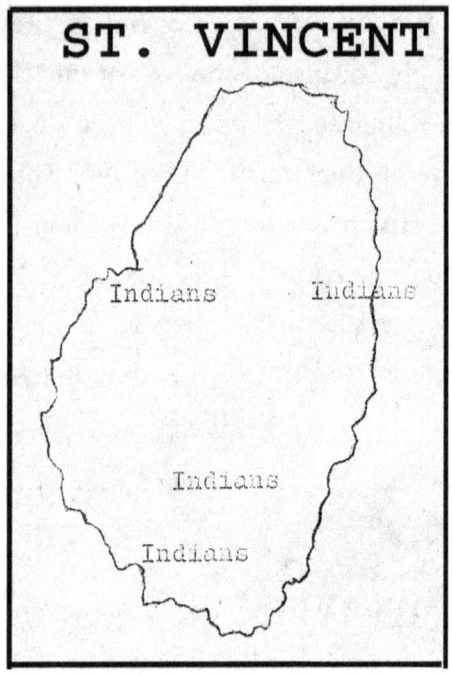

The East Indians in St. Vincent are concentrated in the Rosebank, Calder, Richland Park and Georgetown areas, with some of them in the suburbs of Kingstown. The exact number of East Indians in St. Vincent is not known, but Indians comprise some 5% of the population, which would be approximately 5,000.

The extent to which Indian culture has survived needs first to be investigated quite closely. Indo-Vincentians seem to have learned a great deal about Indian culture from the rest of the Hindu Caribbean, and this complicates the problem of identifying survivals. Many Indians in St. Vincent claim that they are not "real Indians", that the real Indians are the old-timers who had died out. The trend is to regard the Indians of the South Caribbean as being culturally superior. A few old-timers were able to relate quite a lot about life on the plantations in the old days. Generally, it was not much different from plantation life in the rest of the Caribbean.

Indian foods are not common in St. Vincent today. But many people do seem to know about them. One 84 year-old informant said that in the early days of indentureship they had local food, so they did not bother about Indian food. He stressed, however, that food such as roti had been brought over by the first indentures.

Church and State did a good job of deculturation. There are few Indian names surviving and even at the turn of the century most Indians had been Christianized and given Christian names.   Indian culture was kept alive by the pundits-one of whom came from Trinidad - and when the pundits died, Indian culture declined.

There is some kind of social relationships among some Indian families, but there is also an obvious problem of disorganization among the general Indian population. Some time ago, an attempt was made to form an Indian organization, but this, it appears, was mainly for the purpose of playing cricket. Several informants said it did not include rural and poor Indians.

The Indo Vincentians seem to recognize the problems they face. Several acts of discrimination were pointed out to me. I was told of a sign on a door in a garage on Back St. in Kingstown which says "No Indians Allowed." Marriages among Indians is frowned upon. One informant claimed that an Indian girl could not walk the streets of Kingstown with an Indian boy because she would be laughed at.

The rationale for racial discrimination in St. Vincent puzzles the Indians there. One of them writes.... "We always seem to get justified reasons for hostility directed against Indians, whether in East Africa where thousands of Indians were dispossessed and kicked out of Kenya, Tanzania and Uganda penniless, or where we were attacked, and our children were raped and murdered in Wismar, Guyana.

One of the theories put forward is that after all, Indians have so much wealth and they might control the economies and perhaps the politics of the country they have only recently cared to live in, and since the negroes are afraid of being made slaves again, it is only natural that they should fight oppression .

In St. Vincent, Indians are by and large powerless. They do not control any means of production, nor is their number significant, and yet hostilities are directed against them.

One only has to be going somewhere, anytime to be shouted at, "LOOK THE COOLIE!"

Indians are hated simply because they are Indians. Racial hatred has no basis for its continuation.

It is significant that the Governor of the island (a lawyer who worked for the United Nations, travelled to Europe, America, Africa and Asia) could stand up in a graduation ceremony where three Indians had taken honours in the exam and say, "I don't know what our boys are doing." If these boys are not "our boys" whose boys are they? It is a pity that we, who have toiled for these places, giving our blood, sweat and tears should be treated with such contempt.

As in St. Lucia there is a general hostility towards everything Indian. Any attempt at organization had to be made made with great care because of the "jealousy of the blacks." There seems to be a new interest in Indian culture among the young. The new attitude is typified by one bahin who has decided to wear a sari at her wedding in spite of the protests of the church.

....

COMMMENTARY

ELECTORAL OFFICE FRAUD

A Trinidad magistrate recently condemned the Elections and Boundaries Commission for its downright dishonesty in issuing an identity card to a small islander, who is not a citizen of Trinidad and Tobago.

What the magistrate does not know is that some 250,000 of these small islanders have been imported in the last few years and made instant electors, in order to get a black majority at the polls and in the society. If the Commission has any integrity it would immediately investigate this case.

THE MODERN GIRL

By Vijay Mandreker Bahall

Not too long ago I happened to meet a modestly dressed middle-aged lady near the University car park. She came up to me and asked for someone I did not know and then, to my surprise commented,"But you all have a lot of modern girls here".

I was surprised and asked her what she meant.

She replied: "Well out there in the car park I saw a boy and kissing."

"Is that all?"

"No they are... "

"Then you have not seen much yet".

She walked away muttering,"The young generation, eh, the young gen-er-ation."

I did not get the opportunity to discuss with her my own views on the subject, but her remark about the modern girl made me think. I now propose to discuss the subject in two parts: the modern girl and the modern Indian girl.

The modern girl is flooded with special delusions and suggestions from every side. They advertise themselves to get attention like in the movies. They are versed in modern literature of the type which leads to sensual stimulation. The songs they sing and listen to are full of sex and leave little room for creative thought. To achieve popularity in crowded society they feel that they must engage in sexual intimacies. They do not see the need to wait for marriage.

The modern Indian girl thinks that hiding her Eastern culture behind a western front is being modern. She believes that the more westernised she becomes the more modern she will be... so she goes to the extreme.

In clothes she thinks that the more body she exposes, the more modern she is, so she walks about in micro-mini, halter-tops etc. In fact a young girl remarked she wears her clothes even shorter than her western counterparts, who ironically, are realising the sedateness and beauty of the eastern dress, particularly the sari. Thus the Indian girl who goes all the way in dress and also in sex becomes a laughing stock.

We see that although she is popular both with boys and girls and has adopted the western wax of life completely, if she comes from a religious background there is a feeling of extreme guilt on her part because she considers herself 'low class' and not worthy of being 'modern'. The way of life that she has adopted is completely different from the life in which she was brought up.

At times there will be emotional conflicts, especially where her religious ideas are concerned. This results in frustration, depression. So our 'modern' girl who should be exalting in her modernity, is now unhappy and thinks that it might be better, after all not to be modern, for then at least she will be happy and free from frustration and guilt.

The Indian girl believes that modernity means 'keeping away from scrubbing pots and pans'. She feels that sitting behind a desk with polished nails is being modern. There is a psychological reason for this. Her ancestors had to work extremely hard and they were uneducated. As a result she may think that having an education and working less hard away from the fields and home is being modern.

Again this obsession with being modern may lead, her to do things that are inconsistent with her upbringing. For instance, she may have illicit sexual relations with her boss, who may be married, or to make matters worse may be of another race.

Are the characteristics of such girls pleasant to themselves? Is their behaviour virtuous or socially acceptable? Let us think.

GCIO requests recall
of Indian diplomat

The Guyana Council of Indian Organisations has been protesting against the remarks made by the Indian High Commissioner Dr Gopal Singh at the Asoka Chakra presentation ceremony, and is requesting his immediate recall.

At the presentation of the Asoka Chakra medal to Guyana's Prime Minister, Dr Singh is reported to have made certain flattering remarks about Burnham.

According to the GCIO the High Commissioner's remarks did not bear any relation to reality and has described them as partisan politicking in favour of the ruling PNC regime. It could not not understand, the GCIO says, how the High Commissioner could be unaware of the political, economic and cultural mutilation of the Indo-Guyanese by the PNC .

The GCIO hopes that the Indian Government will respond promptly to the request for the recall of Dr Singh. They say that the people of Guyana and people abroad were deliberately being given the impression that the Government of India had given the award to the Prime Minister and the remarks of the High Commissioner gave substance to the misrepresentation.

GCIO'S LETTER TO DR GOPAL SINGH

In his letter to the High Commissioner, the President Doodnath Singh said:

"The Council concluded that your participation and in particular the manner of it, greatly offended the entire Indian Community. As a Senior Diplomat of a country with which Guyanese Indians have long and cherished ancestral ties, you must know that the efforts of legitimate and indigenous organisations to promote and protect Indian culture are being thwarted.

It must certainly be within your knowledge that centrally directed attempts are being made to create divisions in the Indian community. Yet you make a speech which has only served to compound our difficulties. If perchance your object was to promote the interests of India, we are afraid that our Community will not suffer you to do so in this way at our expense.

We regret therefore, to inform you that it is necessary for us to request your immediate recall and we propose sending a copy of this letter to your Foreign Affairs Minister. It will also be necessary form to inform our people of developments in this matter."

Letter to the Editor of Mirror.

In a letter to the Mirror dated 18/8/74 Shri R Ramkissoon said: "In many of his speeches since his arrival to our country, Dr Singh has made a point of praising integration, a concept which has been practised in India for thousands of years.

The Indo-Guyanese also believe in integration, but as a process in which several peoples of diverse beliefs and backgrounds could live together in harmony politically and otherwise, but still be encouraged and given equal opportunities for separate cultural development.

We do not believe however in an integration which seeks to deculturise large sections of a community, in the hope that something richer will arise from the ashes of destruction. The High Commissioner would do well to recall the language riots in his own country and the events which led to the partition of the Punjab, into a separate state for the Sikhs."

....

COMMENTARY: *WHO ALLYUH TRYING TO FOOL?*

On Thursday 21st November, 1974, at the University of the West Indies, St. Augustine Trinidad, a seminar was held at the JFK Lecture Theatre on the topic "The Role of Culture in the Process of Social Change in the Caribbean." The participants represented such groups as NJAC, URO, and OWTU leaders and UWI. The four participants were all of African origin. Not ONE was an Indian. It is noteworthy to record that Indians make up about 50 % of the population, and apparently, it was considered by the organizers, and the proponents of "Africans and Indians Unite" that Indians have no culture, and as such, they did not appear, or were asked to appear at this seminar. Even the lackeys of Afro-colonialism in the form of the "Mohammed Brothers" were not even there, though they do not hold an Indian viewpoint of Trinidad society of geographically based Indians. The absurdity was carried so far, that although there were Indians in the audience, a negro decided to speak about Indian culture – which he didn't know anything about.

103

The Indian man and Indian woman

Kenneth Sonilal

In the Indian society, the life of the Indian woman is intimately bound up with that of the Indian man as his wife, mother, and daughter. A present we see that many of our women are moving out of occupation in the home and into employment outside the home, and the village. there is no doubt that the Indian woman is intellectually gifted as any other woman, and if she is given equal opportunities and facilities, she can make as much progress or even more than the Indian man.

In the past, parents imposed restrictions on their daughters, and slowed down the progress of the Indian woman. However, education has been widespread, and although there are serious problems of the poverty of most Indian families, many go through great sacrifice to educate their children.

In the years gone by. the life of the Indian woman was in the home, or in the cane fields, gardens and rice fields, where she worked side by side with her husband and children. With education the occupational horizons for the Indian woman have extended considerably , and the Indian woman has found her way into employment in the civil service, teaching profession, as secretaries, and many of them after university education emerge higher levels, and can even be found as lawyers and doctors.

Indian mothers were and still are those who took care of the children and attended weddings and other religious ceremonies in the temples and mosques. She did not have to face the outside world, of life in the cities and towns for the greater part of the working day. She was never faced with the questions "Where am I going? Who am I?". The young Indian woman is now faced with this question and there are few people she can call upon in her own families for advice. Thus she seeks the advice of her friends her own age, who may or may not know the answers for her problems. This has arisen, because at the present time, she is the first generation of the Indian women who have moved out of the life within the home.

The old ideas of early and arranged marriages are fading away, and at the present time, new forms have not been created for young Indians to meet together. In the time of arranged marriages, this was not necessary because there was no need to have these things because parents made these decisions. Young people have come under strong influence of the films of Bollywood as well as Indian films, and they want to make decisions for themselves and choose their own marriage partners.

Yet, are they given the necessary advice as to how they should act and evaluate the person who they want to get married to? The high rate of separations and divorces, the wife beatings and rum drinking by young men, show that all is not right in the Indian society.

As a young person, I want to say that there is much to be corrected in our own society. There are serious shortcomings, and this has resulted because, our older members did not realise that it was necessary to introduce new ideas to the traditional

Indian way of life, and others who knew that they should so something refused to do so because they were stubborn or afraid to do so.

Indian women have been the carriers of religion in our homes, and they have played a very important part in religious ceremonies and observances. But where are the men, when this is taking place? They are in the rumshops or playing cards. The Indian woman has not only carried on the religion to her children, but too much burden has been placed on her shoulders. It is high time that Indian men begin to take on some of this responsibility.

With increasing burdens upon the Indian woman, her husband must get out and so something instead of drinking rum, arguing about religion and politics, and criticising young people who are trying to do something for other young people in the villages.

Whenever young people are trying to do something, the older heads, instead of coming to help us, just begin to stir up trouble and break up what we are trying to do, But these people are few in number and cause a lot of trouble, while others are in sympathy with our cause but are afraid to come out and help us.

In our religion and philosophy, Indian women have been treated with great respect and honour, Sita sits at the side of Raam, and not under his feet. She has been given a position of equality. Lakshmi has been elevated to the position of a goddess, who is worshipped. There are many other examples which I can use, but these are two which everyone knows about and will understand easily.

When one looks around, it is easy to see that many young men treat Indian girls with scant respect and even curse and make bad comments, especially if they have a few drinks. If the Indian society is to progress, we must first regain that respect both for ourselves and our women.

Young Indian boys and girls have been separated, and even when they meet under their parents' eyes they are afraid, some of them, to speak to each other. Everyone is aware of the many secret notes and letters which pass by hand or through friends, in order for boys and girls to get to know each other. This takes place, because they cannot meet in the open and talk to each other. The many bazaars and even the cinema have provided a common place where boys and girls see each other.

Our parents must know that there is is nothing wrong if boys and girls meet and talk and even fall in love and get married. Is it not better to let this happen, than to find one day that your daughter runs away with a boy she likes, or even the greater 'disgrace' of a girl having a baby without being married.

Let us begin to tale a good look at ourselves as young people. and try to not to argue with our parents but to show them reasons why they should try to accept the 'modern ways'. We cannot expect them to change overnight.

As young people who still believe in our dharma, we must decide where we are going, what we want out of life, and how we are going to achieve our aims and carry on the religion and the society when the old ones have died.

Indians in Grenada

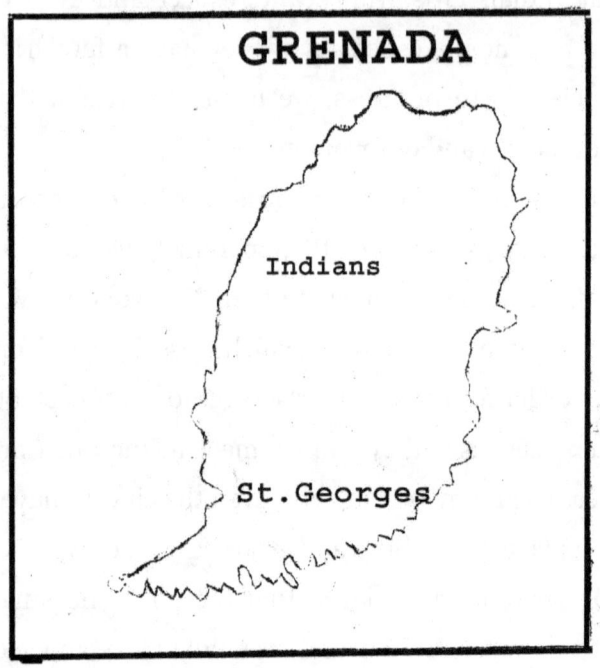

Like the other unfortunate Indians living in small communities in the poverty stricken and neglected islands of the eastern Caribbean, the Indians in Grenada whose numerical estimate can be said to be about 5,000 persons, are in as bad a way as the Indians of St. Lucia, St. Vincent, and Jamaica. The cultural rape of these Indians appears to have reached an alarming rate.

Although Indians, especially women, still pride themselves on their Indian cooking, and the families continue to to tune in their radios to the Indian programs that they could hear from the Trinidad radio stations. Many of them have relatives who have escaped Grenada, and having fled to Trinidad, have immersed themselves into the Trinidad Indian society, and yet show no difference in their outlook and attitude towards life.

Of the Indians in Grenada, A.W. Singham in his book "The Hero and the Crowd", draws the notice of the reader to the fact that Indians are generally looked down upon by the rest of the country and are scornfully called "coolies". It appears that this name was given to the Indians after they were baptized by Caribbean exploitation of the Christian planters in the region.

Reports have indicated that there is a tendency for the Trinidad Indians "elite" that holidays in Grand Anse and other parts of Grenada, to look down on the Grenadian Indians and totally disregard them as other human beings.

Nevertheless it appears that the Presbyterian deculturation process has also been set into action, together with the state and church to bring about the complete extinction of any survival of Indianness among the Grenada Indians.

The Indians in Grenada do look forward to knowing more about Indians in the rest of the Caribbean.

Advice to Indian husbands

It has been drawn to the attention of our magazine,by Indian women, especially young women and newly married doolahins, that their husbands always compare their cooking to their mothers' food, and say that their wives cannot cook. This is well recognized by young girls, that they very often cannot cook as well as their mother-in-laws.

But, to these husbands, you are making a bad comparison, since your mother has cooked 3 x 365 meals per year for the last 25 years, that is a total of 25,000 meals. That makes her an expert, to your wife, who has now started on her first thousand.

Another bad habit drawn to our attention is that when the doolahin makes something, especially an Indian dish, for the first time, and it does not come out perfect, there is a big laugh and the girl is mocked.

`But if we look at it, there are people who make cakes hundreds of times and it falls, with a droop or a hole in the centre. It takes a lot of time, energy and patience to cook Indian food.

Appreciate the trouble your wife has gone through in her first attempt, and encourage her. It will pay off later.

Indians in Surinam

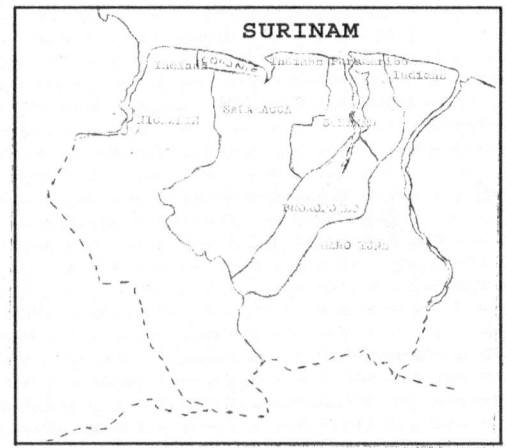

As early as 1855, the Dutch Christian planters of Surinam began to tap new sources of labour by importing emigrants from countries such as Madeira and China. These sources had been used by the British as early as the 1830's, for the Christian owned plantations in the British Caribbean. Like the British, the Dutch failed. Nevertheless the Parliament of the Netherlands abolished slavery on the ninth of July 1862, while the planters looked to a gloomy future with the problem of decreasing labour.

By the 1860's the British planters in the Caribbean had obtained increase prosperity from the brutal exploitation of Indians, while the liberated Negroes continued to be reluctant to work on the plantations. In Surinam, during the period of state supervision of labour from 1862 to 1872, no less than 77 plantations closed down and the acreage of cultivation decreased from 40,929 acres to 25,449 acres. (38 percent of plantation acreage).

However in 1870 the British government decided to give the Dutch planters the right to use Indians will work on their plantations via the devious methods of recruitment, established by the British Christians in India. Depots were also established in Bihar and the United Province (areas from which Indians were also collected by the British paid recruiters, "the scum of the earth", for the British Caribbean. Like the slave trade, the recruiters were paid per head of man, as when one carries goats to the slaughterhouse. From 1873 to 1916, the number of Indians shipped to Suriname was 34,304. For 70 percent of them, there was not the five-year contract of their employment, but "enslavement" for their lives and the lives of their children and grandchildren.

Although many of them have escaped plantation labour and have established as small peasant farmers, many are still trapped in the poverty of plantation exploitation. The more fortunate Indians have secured important positions at the lower rung of the economic ladder-in small farming, the cultivation of vegetables, cattle rearing in the neighborhood of Paramaribo, the transportation system and market trading, small shopkeepers, tailors and other small trades.

On this economic base, their children have moved into primary and secondary education. There has been an increasing number of them who are secondary schooled and university trained-since special value in the Indian family, is placed on testimonials, reports, diplomas and academic titles. An increasing number have begun to enter the professions. The Indians of Surinam have been more fortunate in cultural retention since the Dutch, being more liberal and having a more civilized approach approach to another culture (so unlike the narrow minded British) have allowed the teaching of Hindustani (a mixture of Hindi and Urdu).

In the British Caribbean the teaching of Hindustani has been banned in primary and secondary schools by fascist educational systems. Both Hindu and Muslim religions have orthodox and 'modernist' subgroups. In politics, the Moslems and Hindus have combined to form the United Indian Party (Verenidge Hindostaanse Partij), designated V.H.P. The formation of political parties has lee to an increased ethnic consciousness. "Hum Hindustani Hai" (We are Indians) finds its expression in the party.

Vidia Naipaul writes in "Middle Passage", a book he wrote in 1961, of Surinam..." it does not have the racial problems of these territories (British Guiana and Trinidad), though there is inevitably a growing rivalry between Negroes and East Indians, the two largest groups. With Dutch realism the Surinamers have avoided racial collision not by ignoring group differences but by openly acknowledging them. The political parties are racial, but the government is a coalition of these parties."

Speckman, in his book on East Indians and Surinam, page 115-116, draws reference to a debate on 'inter-racial marriage'. Speckman writes,"When this debate came to an end the creole exclaimed,"We shall end by forcing your group to become assimilated.". As to assimilation, Naipaul writes, in "Middle Passage", page 165. "Racial equality and assimilation are attractive, but only underline the loss, since to accept assimilation is in a way to accept permanent inferiority."

The Indian in Surinam, like the Indian in the rest of the Caribbean, is at present faced with this problem of the growth of this trend to enforce a status of inferiority upon them by the rising tide of Afro-colonialism and Afro-fascism in the Caribbean. Such forms are most clearly seen in those territories where the percentage of the population of Indians is under 5% of the total population. Even in Guyana and Trinidad, where the Indians total about one half of the population. We also find this destructive activity being perpetrated on the Indians of Guyana, Trinidad and Surinam.

....

COMMENTARY: GOWANDAN RESIGNS; TWO AND A HALF CHEERS

Super-marxist, anti-Indian Krishna Gowandan, arch-enemy of Indians and everything Indian has resigned from the TIWU. But not before he revealed that there were certain officers in the union who are anti-Indian. Perhaps, if Gowandan had stayed on 12 more years he would have found out that the whole union is anti-Indian and hence the reason why only Indian workers are being retrenched. If he had stayed on for 24 years he would have found that the whole society is anti-Indian. With insight as with everything else: better late than never.

www.ingramcontent.com/pod-product-compliance
Lightning Source LLC
Chambersburg PA
CBHW072207280526
45788CB00002B/917